ARIZONA HIKING WITH KIDS

50 Hiking Adventures for Families

By
Bridge Press

Bridge Press
Support@BridgePress.org

Copyright 2021. Bridge Press LLC. All Rights Reserved.
No part of this book may be reproduced or transmitted in any form or by any means, electronic or mechanical, including photocopying, recording or by any other form without written permission from the publisher.

ISBN: 978-1-955149-31-0

FREE BONUS

Find Out 31 Incredible Places You Can Visit Next! Just Go To:

purplelink.org/travel

TABLE OF CONTENTS

FREE BONUS 3
Introduction: Hiking with Kids 1
About Arizona 8
Landscape and Climate 9
Butcher Jones Trail - Saguaro Lake 10
Hidden Valley - South Mountain Park 12
Hole in the Rock - Papago Park 14
Hieroglyphic Trail - Superstition Wilderness 16
Jewel of the Creek & Dragonfly Loop 18
McDowell Mountain North Trail 20
Jojoba Trail - Bartlett Lake 22
Roadrunner Trail - Lake Pleasant 24
Go John-Quartz-Slate Loop - Cave Creek Regional Park 26
White Tank Waterfall Trail - White Tank Mountains 28
Usery Mountain Regional Park 30
Kachina Hiking Trail - San Francisco Mountains 32
Lookout Mountain Trails - Phoenix Mountain Preserve 34
Veit Springs Trail 36
Montezuma Castle National Monument Trail 38
Pine & Gowan Hiking Trail Loop 40
Soldier Pass Trail - Sedona 42
Cathedral Rock Trail 44
Water Wheel & Ellison Creek Cascades 46
Badger Springs 48
Lynx Lake Loop Trail 50
Watson Lake Loop 52
Willow Lake Loop 54
Dead Horse Ranch Lagoon Loop 56
Coconino Lava River Cave 58
Lyman Lake State Park 60
Granite Gardens at Watson Lake Park 62
Red Mountain Trail 64
Broken Arrow Trail 66
Bell Rock Pathway Trail 68

See Spring Trail	70
Hayden Butte Preserve & "A" Mountain	72
Cibecue Falls - Cibecue Creek Trail	74
Devil's Bridge Trail	76
Treasure Loop Trail - Lost Dutchman State Park	78
Cape Royal Trail at Grand Canyon National Park	80
Crystal Forest Trail at Petrified Forest National Park	82
Hanging Garden Trail at Glen Canyon National Recreation Area	84
Lava Flow Trail at Sunset Crater Volcano National Monument	86
Signal Hill - Saguaro National Park	88
Seven Falls Trail	90
Sugarloaf Loop Trail	92
Grand Canyon South Rim Trail	94
Fay Canyon Trail	96
Fossil Creek Waterfall	98
Horseshoe Bend Trail	100
White Pocket - Vermillion Cliffs	102
Moonlight-Stargazer- San Tan Trail	104
Pinnacle Peak	106
The Wind Cave Trail in East Mesa	108

INTRODUCTION: HIKING WITH KIDS

Hiking with family and/or friends brings everyone closer together and makes memories to cherish for years to come. To ensure you get the most out of the experience, we've compiled fifty trails and locations in Arizona that are suitable for kids in your life to tag along.

Each entry features a family-friendly location and hikes to explore, along with useful information to know before you go. Check out the descriptions to preview what to expect, the best times to go, passes/permits/fees required, amenities available, directions to the destination, what to pack, and what to keep an eye out for in terms of wildlife, landmarks, fossils, or other interesting features.

Following each information page is a map of the featured hike for your convenience. Before embarking on your adventures, take a look at these tips for hiking with kids, so you're prepared for every scenario.

Tips for Hiking with Kids
Plan Ahead
For any hike, consider the time of day/year and weather conditions of the area. Dress everyone in layers. Starting out in the morning is ideal to avoid the extreme Arizona heat in the warmer months, and you will also avoid the crowds at popular sites. Also, some trails or areas are not accessible when wet, so it is best to check the forecast and trail conditions. Arizona is prone to fire danger and sudden thunderstorms during the monsoon season of the summer.

With kids especially, plan for breaks or energy stops along the way, in shady areas, if possible. Kids will enjoy themselves more if they are rested and fed along the way. Bathroom breaks are important to plan as well, and you will find information about restrooms available in the amenities section of each entry.

For your first hikes, pick something short and easy with features such as bodies of water or other interesting landmarks. Keeping the kids engaged and easing them into hiking will provide an enjoyable experience for all.

Always stay on the trails and prepare for any potential encounters with wildlife such as scorpions, snakes, and other critters. It is generally best to not wear open shoes on hikes in Arizona. Don't rely on GPS and electronic devices — have a physical map with you.

Age Considerations
Infants (0-12 months) - Practice walking with the child in their carrier (backpack or sling). You may wish to start the trail at naptime. The motion of your moving will likely lull a baby to sleep, and it's best to avoid disrupting their sleep routine. Easy (1-2) trails recommended.

Toddlers/Young Kids (1-4 years) - At this age, you can start letting them toddle along on the hike, but also be prepared to carry your tot at some point along the way. Also, embrace the dirt because they are going to get dirty. Easy to moderate (1-3) trails recommended.

Grade School (5-12 years) - When first starting, set rules such as staying within sight, which can be relaxed as they become more responsible. Give the child a safety whistle and teach them to properly use it. This age will enjoy destinations with activity potential, such as scrambling over boulders. Older kids might also appreciate bringing along friends. Easy to moderate trails (1-4) recommended.

Make it Fun!
Kids love engagement, and there are many ways to keep your hike extra fun. Make a game out of the experience, such as watching for certain signs of wildlife, creating a scavenger hunt, establishing checkpoints or achievements, singing songs, or a round of "I Spy."

Hiking in many areas offers opportunities to educate everyone about the history, geology, and wildlife of the area, and you can educate young ones about "leave no trace" and hiking responsibly.

Consider designating a leader in your group and rotate so everyone has a turn to lead. If they're old enough, you can even teach them to read the map. Also, kids love having their own gear, even if it's a small pack to carry their water bottle and a snack.

Reinforce good behaviors and accomplishments with words of encouragement and praise. Keep it interactive and have fun!

What to Bring
For hiking at any age, you should always have "The 10 Essentials," which are: navigation (map/GPS), a headlamp with spare batteries, sun protection (sunscreen, hats, sunglasses), a first aid kit, a knife/multi-tool, means to start and sustain a fire, emergency shelter (*e.g.,* plastic tube tent), extra food, extra water, and extra clothes.

Additional items: binoculars, battery packs, spray bottles, bug repellent, camera, extra socks, swimsuits, floaties/life preservers, towels, fishing gear, camping gear, cooking utensils/cookout supplies, umbrellas, wet wipes, tissues, lip balm, magnifying glass, field guides, safety whistle, waste bags, and family-favorite snacks.

Best Hikes Breakdown

Best Desert Hikes

- Horseshoe Bend Trail
    - 1.4 miles, easy (1), high view of the Colorado River
- Devil's Bridge Trail
    - 2 miles, easy (2), huge red rock arch
- The Wind Cave Trail in East Mesa
    - 3 miles, easy (2)
- Crystal Forest Trail at Petrified Forest National Park
    - 0.75 miles, easy (1), petrified wood and crystals
- Moonlight-Stargazer-San Tan Trail
    - 2.3 miles, easy (2), customizable

Best Lake Hikes

- Butcher Jones Trail at Saguaro Lake
    - 4 miles, easy (1), tour boat cruise available
- Roadrunner Trail - Lake Pleasant
    - 1.6 miles, easy (1), lake access
- Jojoba Trail - Bartlett Lake
    - 2.7 miles, easy (1)
- Willow Lake Loop
    - 5.2 miles, one side is easy (1), one side is moderate (2.5)
- Watson Lake Loop

- 4.8 miles of trail segments, easy-moderate (1-3), customizable, Granite Dells

Best Waterfall Hikes

- White Tank Waterfall Trail - White Tank Mountains
    - 1.8 miles, easy (1), partially paved

- Water Wheel & Ellison Creek Cascades
    - 1.8 miles, easy (1), swimming hole

- Seven Falls Trail
    - 4.6 miles, moderate (2.5), tram trip

- Fossil Creek Waterfall
    - 1 mile, easy (1), swimming hole

- Cibecue Falls - Cibecue Creek Trail
    - 3 miles, moderate (3), small cave, rugged trail

Best Mountain Hikes

- Lookout Mountain Trails - Phoenix Mountain Preserve
    - 0.9 miles to the summit, rated moderate (3), also a 2.2-mile trail around the mountain, rated easy (2)

- Red Mountain Trail
    - 2.7 miles, easy (1), cinder volcano

- Hayden Butte Preserve & "A" Mountain
    - 1.7 miles, easy (2), Giant "A" for University of Arizona

- Treasure Loop Trail - Lost Dutchman State Park
    - 2.4 miles, easy (2), views of Superstition Mountains

- Signal Hill - Saguaro National Park
    - 0.4 miles, easy (1), petroglyphs

Best Canyon Hikes

- Cape Royal Trail at Grand Canyon National Park
    - 0.3 miles, easy (1), stroller accessible

- Grand Canyon South Rim Trail
    - 8 miles, bus stops along the way, easy (2)

- Badger Springs
    - Less than a mile, easy (1), swimming holes

Best Historic Hikes

- Hieroglyphs Trail in Superstition Wilderness
    - 2.9 miles, moderate (3), petroglyphs

- Veit Springs
    - 1.6 miles, easy (1), old pioneer cabin

- Montezuma Castle National Monument Trail
    - 1/3 mile, easy (1), huge cliff dwelling, and well

- Lyman Lake State Park
    - 3 trails, all less than 1 mile, easy (1-2), petroglyphs, ruins

Best Hikes Near Phoenix

- Hidden Valley in South Mountain Park
    - 3.6 miles, moderate (3), dog-friendly, rock tunnel

- Hole in the Rock at Papago Park

    - 0.3 miles, easy (1), near the zoo

- Jewel of the Creek & Dragonfly Loop
    - 2 miles, easy (2)

- McDowell Mountain North Trail
    - 2.9 miles, easy (2), self-guided tour with destinations

- Pinnacle Peak
    - 3.5 miles, easy (2), rock climbing

ABOUT ARIZONA

Arizona is a four-corner state, which is a region shared with Utah, Colorado, and New Mexico. The state's name seems to originate from its previous Spanish name, *Arizonac*, derived from the O'odham name *ali sonak*, which means "small spring." This initially only applied to an area near the silver mines of Planchas de Plata, Sonora.

Officially nicknamed "The Grand Canyon State," Arizona is known for being home to one of the Seven Wonders of the World, the Grand Canyon National Park. It is the only Wonder of the World located in the United States.

Native to the Sonoran Desert of Arizona, the saguaro cactus is the largest cactus in the world. A saguaro (pronounced "suh-wah-roe") can grow to be 40-60 feet tall, and you will encounter them on many of the hikes in this book. Arizona's state flower is the saguaro blossom, which appears on the tips of the cactus's arms in the spring.

Home to a diverse population, about one-quarter of Arizona is Indian reservations of twenty-seven Native American tribes. The largest federally recognized Native American tribe in Arizona is the Navajo Nation.

As the state that produces the most copper in the U.S., Arizona is also known as the "Copper State." There are twenty-two national parks and monuments in Arizona, so there is a lot to see. It is the sixth-largest state by area and the fourteenth most populous. Arizona achieved statehood on February 14, 1912, and was the last of the contiguous states to be admitted to the Union.

LANDSCAPE AND CLIMATE

Arizona is a large area with variations in elevation and hosts a variety of landscapes and climate conditions. As a state in the Southwest U.S., Arizona contains high mountains, the Colorado Plateau, and mesas.

It is a mostly arid climate, but 27 percent of the state is forest, with forests of pine, Douglas fir, and spruce trees. In fact, the world's largest stand of ponderosa pine trees is in Arizona.

There are several mountain ranges, such as the San Francisco Mountains, along with large, deep canyons. Northern Arizona is home to the Grand Canyon. Carved by the Colorado River, the Grand Canyon is 277 miles long, with widths ranging from 4 to 18 miles, and gets as deep as 1 mile.

The Desert Basin and Range region in the southern portion of Arizona feature topography shaped by prehistoric volcanism. This landscape is full of xerophytic plants like the cactus.

Southern Arizona is a desert climate, with very hot summers and mild winters. Northern Arizona is moderate in the summer and produces an abundance of snow in the winter.

There are two rainy seasons in Arizona — winter when cold fronts come from the Pacific Ocean and a monsoon in the summer. The North American monsoon (also known as the Southwest monsoon, the Mexican monsoon, the New Mexico monsoon, or the Arizona monsoon) typically occurs between July and September.

BUTCHER JONES TRAIL - SAGUARO LAKE

Formed by the Stewart Mountain Dam, the Saguaro Lake is built on the Salt River and is found in the Tonto National Forest. With 22 miles of shoreline, there's plenty of space for families to swim, boat, kayak, sail, jet ski, fish, and camp. The Butcher Jones Trail starts near the edge of the lake, is suitable for all skill levels, and is rated easy (2) at a total of 4 miles round trip. There's also a tour boat that offers a cruise narrated by a coast-guard-certified captain called The Desert Belle if you'd prefer to explore via water.

Best time to visit: Spring and summer

Pass/permit/fees: $8 Tonto Daily Pass/$4 watercraft sticker per watercraft. Desert Bell Tickets are $24 for 12 and older, $15 for ages 3-12, and $5 for under 3.

Amenities: Restrooms, water, restaurants, picnic tables, boat ramps, and the Maricopa County Sheriff's aid station are all located at the Saguaro del Norte.

How to get there: From Mesa, AZ, travel 27 miles north on State Hwy. 87 to Bush Hwy. for 2.5 miles to Butcher Jones Beach Rd. Turn left and travel 2 miles to the Butcher Jones Recreational Area. The trailhead is in the southeast corner of the parking lot.

What to pack: Sunscreen, swimsuits, binoculars, camping gear

Can you find? Bodies of water attract birds, so keep your eyes out for bald eagles, osprey, peregrine falcons, Harris's hawks, and herons in this area. If you're lucky, you might also encounter river otters.

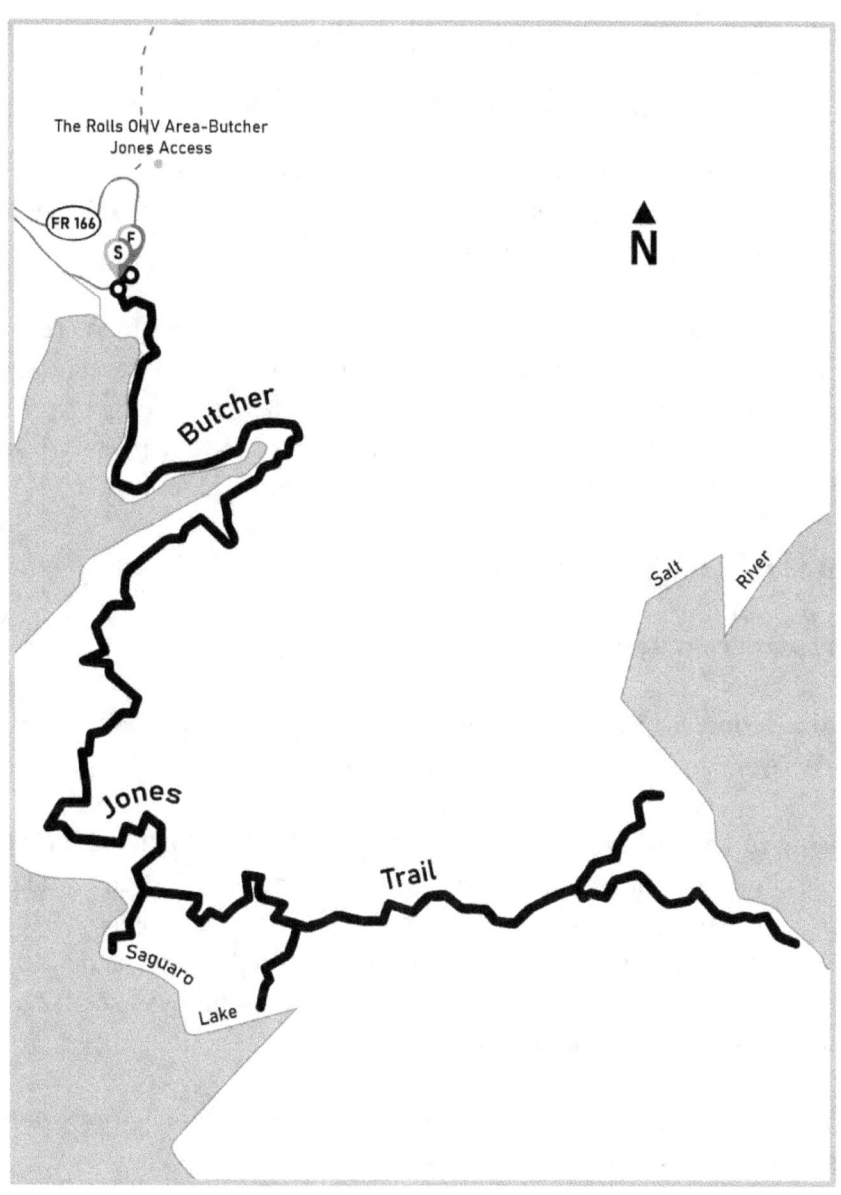

HIDDEN VALLEY - SOUTH MOUNTAIN PARK

South Mountain Park is the largest municipal park in the U.S. and one of the largest urban parks in the world. The Hidden Valley via Mormon Trail is a popular one for families.

A rock tunnel is a highlight of the trail and provides shade for a break. Near the end of the trail is Fat Man's Pass, a narrow slit between two massive boulders. Featuring city panoramas and unique rock formations, the trail is 3.6 miles and rated moderate (3). There is a 918-elevation gain, and dogs are welcome.

Best time to visit: Spring, fall, winter

Pass/permit/fees: No pass, permit, or fee required

Amenities: Restrooms available around the park but not on the trail. There are also picnic areas with grills in the park.

How to get there: From Phoenix, take the 1-10 East and exit off of Baseline/Guadalupe (exit 155) and turn right onto Baseline. Take Baseline straight for 3.6 miles then turn left onto 24th St. Follow 24th St. down for about .8 mile. Access the Mormon Trailhead from the 24th St. Trailhead. Hike up the Mormon Trail 1.5 miles until you see a sign pointing to Hidden Valley Tunnel.

What to pack: Sunscreen, hat, sunglasses, hiking boots/shoes (rocky, steep in places), water, food

Can you find? Keep an eye on the trail for scampering lizards such as the chuckwalla. Count how many saguaro cacti you see, and check for petroglyphs on the stone walls around you.

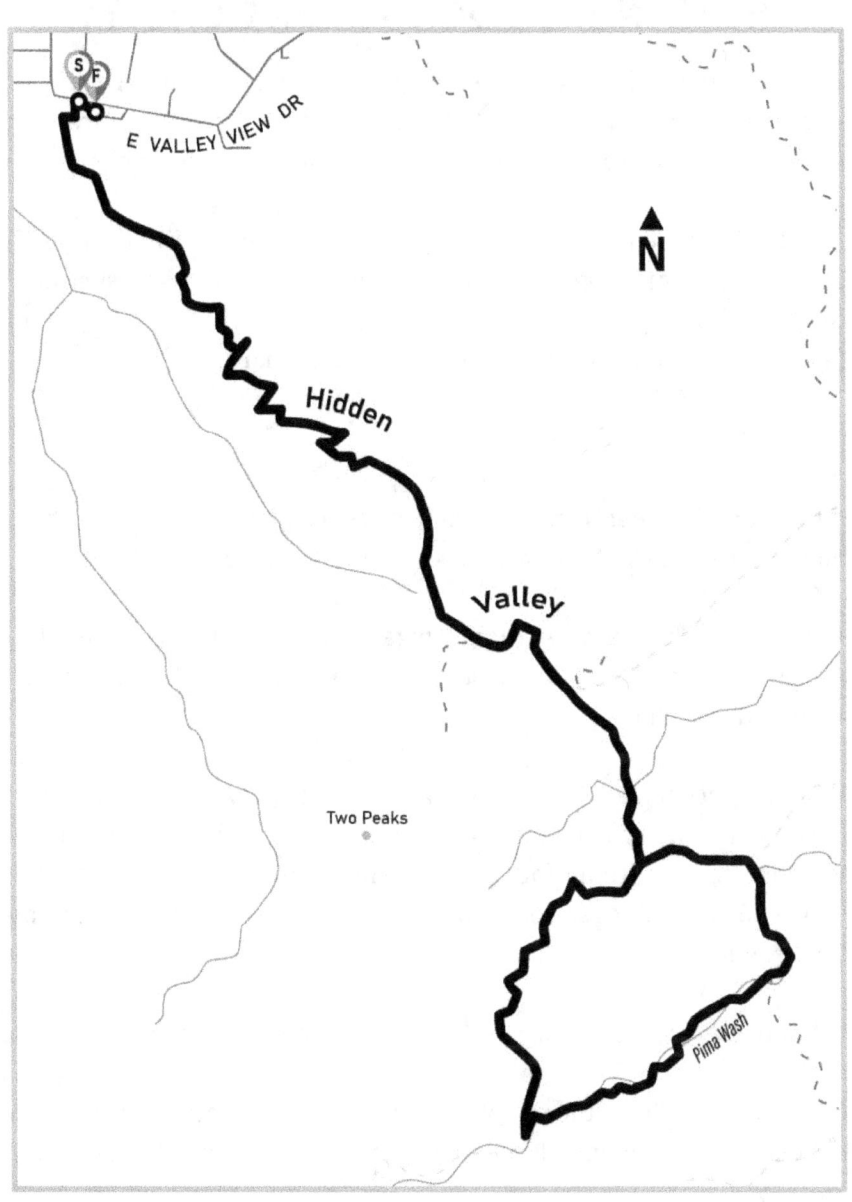

HOLE IN THE ROCK - PAPAGO PARK

The kids can climb rocks and enjoy great views of the park, red rocks, and downtown Phoenix from the top of the trail. The main attraction is the Hole in the Rock formation found at the end of the trail.

A short, 0.3-mile hike, this trail is great for beginners, rated easy (1), and also nice for all ages. Two little lakes and various trails surround the hike should you wish to extend your adventure. For a full day of family fun, the Phoenix Zoo is next door to the park.

Best time to visit: October-April

Pass/permit/fees: No pass, permit, or fee required. There are fishing holes in the area, but you will need a fishing license.

Amenities: There are restrooms in gated parking areas and near the ranger station. There are also shaded ramadas and picnic areas around the lagoons.

How to get there: From Phoenix, on AZ-202, exit onto Priest Dr. heading north. Drive for 1.3 miles and turn right at the entrance to the Phoenix Zoo. Continue for 500 feet and turn left onto Papago Rd., which becomes Ranger Loop Trail, and drive 0.5 miles to the parking lot for the trail.

What to pack: Sunscreen, snacks, water, camera, fishing gear

Can you find? From the top of the trail, look at downtown Phoenix in the distance. You might also see jackrabbits or hummingbirds on your journey.

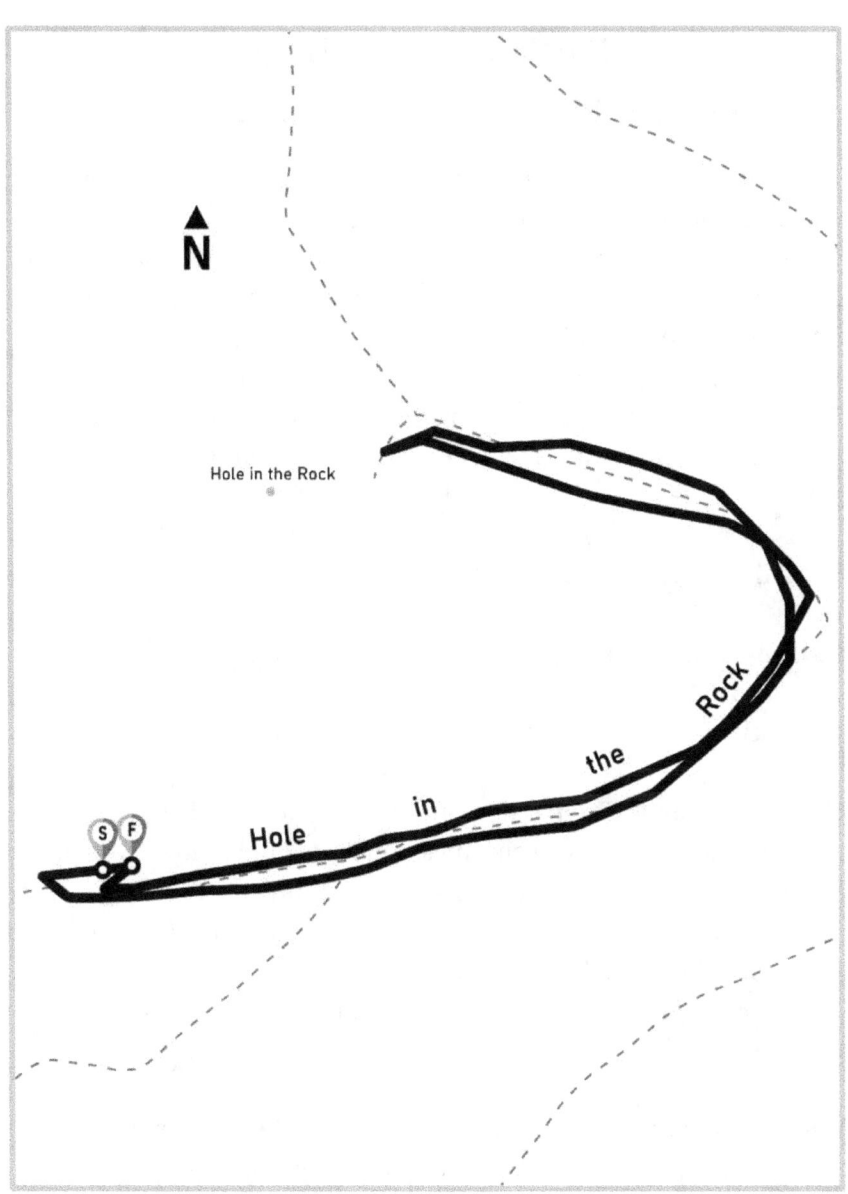

HIEROGLYPHIC TRAIL - SUPERSTITION WILDERNESS

This day hike through the Hieroglyphic Canyon rewards hikers with views of mountains, canyons, pools, and ancient petroglyphs. The trail was somewhat misnamed by early Europeans. Hieroglyphs are from Egypt, but these are rock carvings etched by an ancient tribe called the Hohokam from up to 1500 years ago.

Enjoy the long-distance views over Gold Canyon and close-ups of the Superstition Mountains and Wilderness. The trail is 2.9 miles round trip, moderate (3), and a great educational opportunity.

Best time to visit: Winter

Pass/permit/fees: No pass, permit, or fee required.

Amenities: Restrooms facilities at the trailhead

How to get there: From Gold Canyon, AZ, follow US 60 East to South Kings Ranch Rd. Turn left on Kings Ranch Rd. and follow 2.8 miles to Baseline. Turn right on Baseline and continue 0.2 miles. Follow Baseline left where it becomes Mohican Rd. and follow 0.4 miles to Valleyview Rd. Turn left onto Valleyview and continue onto S. White Tail. Turn right onto Cloudview Rd. and continue 0.4 miles to the trailhead parking area.

What to pack: It's a bit rocky, so wear good hiking boots. There is no shade, so bring sunscreen, hats, sunglasses, and water, snacks.

Can you find? Saguaro, barrel cacti, and teddy bear cholla are common in the desert. How many ancient petroglyphs can you see?

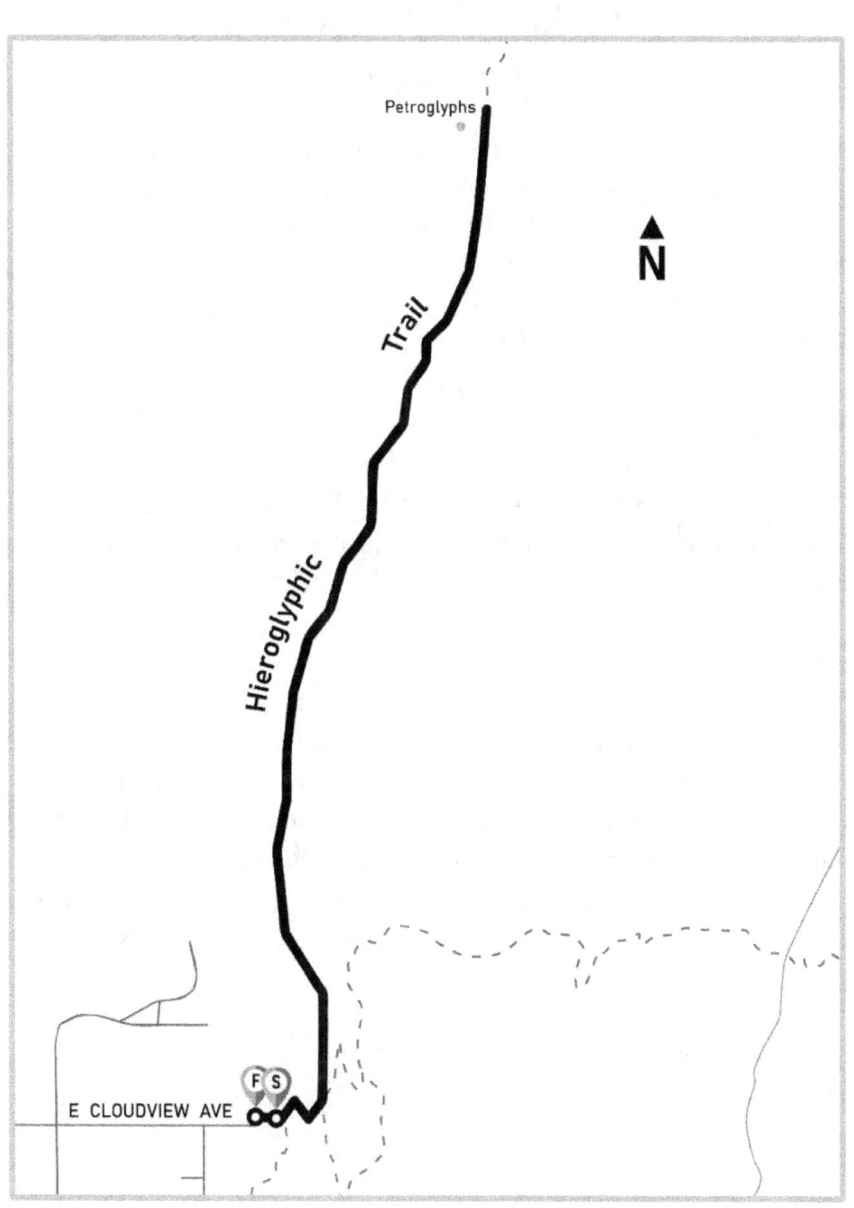

JEWEL OF THE CREEK & DRAGONFLY LOOP

A desert oasis, the Jewel of the Creek and Dragonfly Loop Trail hosts abundant desert flora and wildlife. This easy (2), two-mile loop is great for beginners and all ages with many trees and much shade. The trail circles the banks of Cave Creek, and there's a pond along the way, too. The small cave and wood plank bridges over crossing the creek make this an adventurous hike for kids.

Best time to visit: Spring - early fall

Pass/permit/fees: No pass, permit, or fee required for parking at Jewel of Creek parking lot. $2 fee to park in the Spur Cross parking area down the road.

Amenities: No restrooms at trail

How to get there: From Phoenix, AZ, take Hwy. 10.5 miles to Cave Creek Rd. Turn left and continue for 1.4 miles to North Fleming Springs Rd. and turn left. Over the next ¾ mile, the road becomes North Echo Canyon Dr., then North Sierra Vista Rd., and then North Cottonwood Canyon Rd. Continue 8.5 miles to Spur Cross Rd., turn left, and continue for 1 mile. The parking lot is on the left, across from the riding stable.

What to pack: Bring a flashlight for the cave and water. It can get muddy, so bring extra clothes, socks, and good shoes if it's rained recently.

Can you find? The water draws butterflies and dragonflies to the area. There might even be minnows in the creek. If you see a giant desert centipede, enjoy it from a distance.

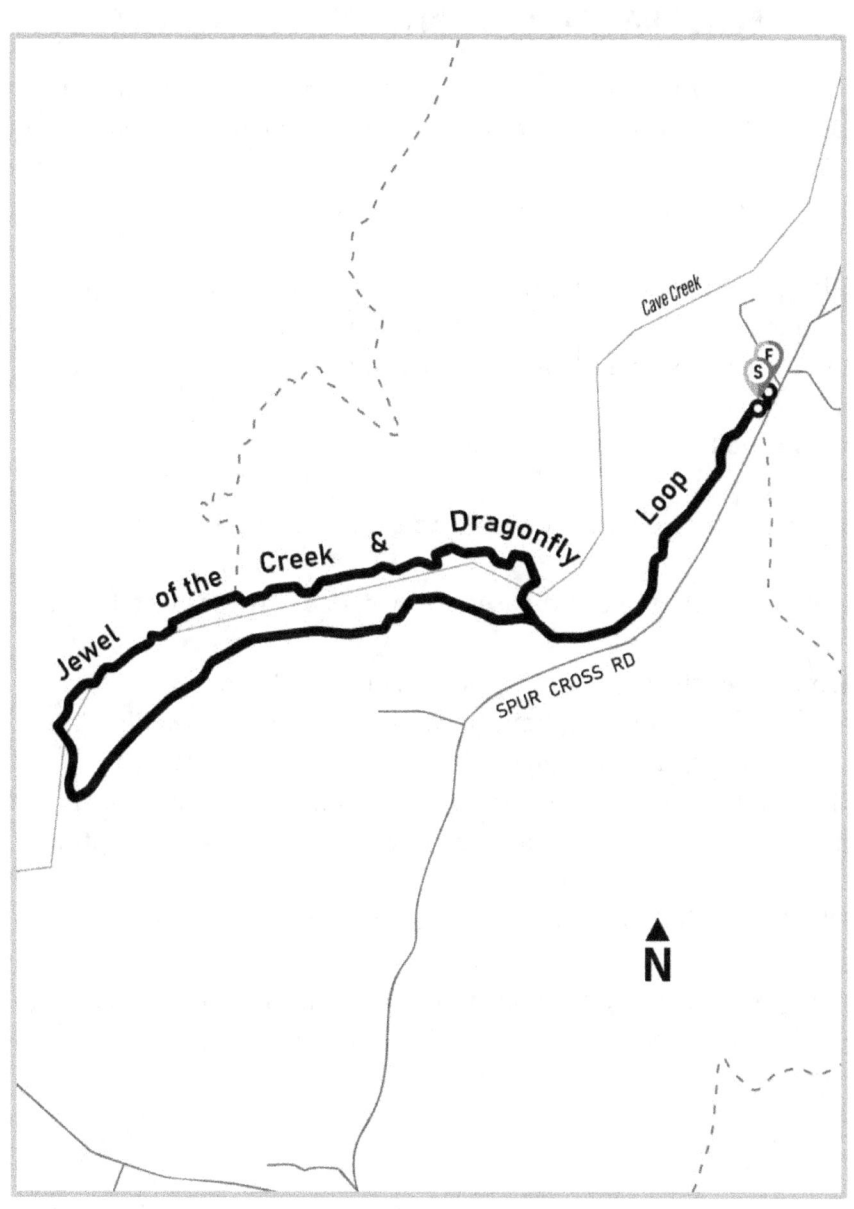

MCDOWELL MOUNTAIN NORTH TRAIL

The North Trail located in the McDowell Mountain Regional Park is a self-guided tour that is perfect for kids. It is a flat, easy (1) loop trail of 2.9 miles. There is also a nature center near the entrance of the park that is worth visiting to see some wildlife on display.

Along the trail, there are thirty-four marker posts that correspond to a sheet you can pick up at the registration desk. Information about the area is featured at each destination along the way.

Best time to visit: March-October

Pass/permit/fees: $7 per vehicle day-use entry fee

Amenities: Portable outhouses are available at the trailhead.

How to get there: From Phoenix, AZ, take AZ-202 east to SR 87/Beeline Hwy. Continue northeast on SR 87 to Shea Blvd. Travel west on Shea Blvd. to Saguaro Blvd.; turn north. Continue through the town of Fountain Hills to Fountain Hills Blvd. Turn right and travel 4 miles to the McDowell Mountain Regional Park entrance.

What to pack: Water, snacks, sunscreen, hats, sunglasses

Can you find? Look for all thirty-four information markers that describe the cacti, mountains, wildlife, and include desert trivia.

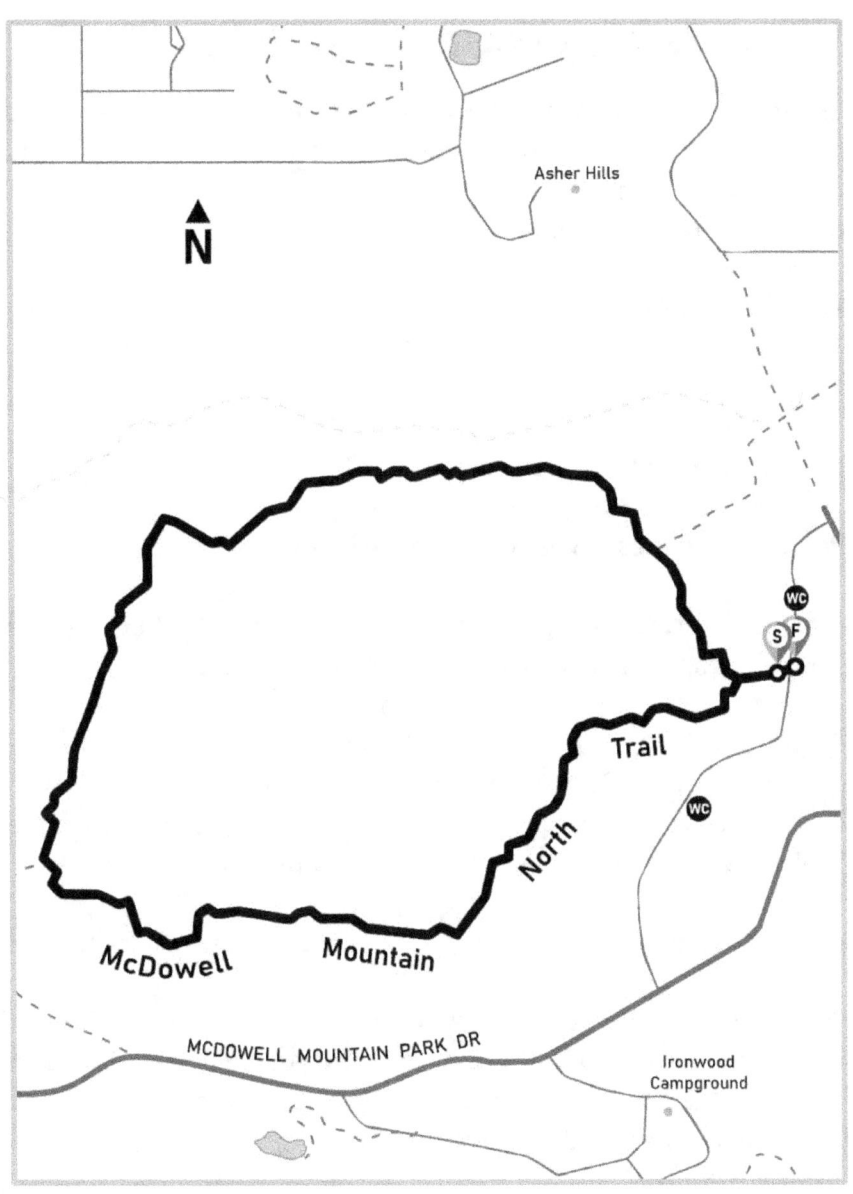

JOJOBA TRAIL - BARTLETT LAKE

Created by the damming of the Verde River, the Bartlett Lake Marina has 2,815 acres of boatable surface area. The water is pristine and great for swimming, fishing, water skiing, and wakeboarding. Camping is available around the shoreline.

The Jojoba Trail is 2.7 miles, rated easy (1), and great for all skill levels. The trail ends at Rattlesnake Cove Beach if you want to stay and take a dip in the lake.

Best time to visit: Spring or fall

Pass/permit/fees: $6 per vehicle per day, $4 per watercraft

Amenities: Private and public restrooms available. The Dock Store is stocked with beverages, snacks, accessories, and apparel.

How to get there: From Phoenix, AZ, take I-17 N to exit 223, Carefree Hwy., keep left on Cave Creek Road, then turn right on Bartlett Dam Rd. until you reach the park entrance. Access the Jojoba Trail from the Jojoba boating parking lot inside the park by the lake.

What to pack: Water, hats, sunglasses, sunscreen, swimsuits, towels

Can you find? If you see a deer with huge ears, it's likely a mule deer. Bald eagles are known to fly overhead, and you might smell javelina before you see them. Check out the saguaro, mesquite trees, and ocotillo in the surrounding landscape.

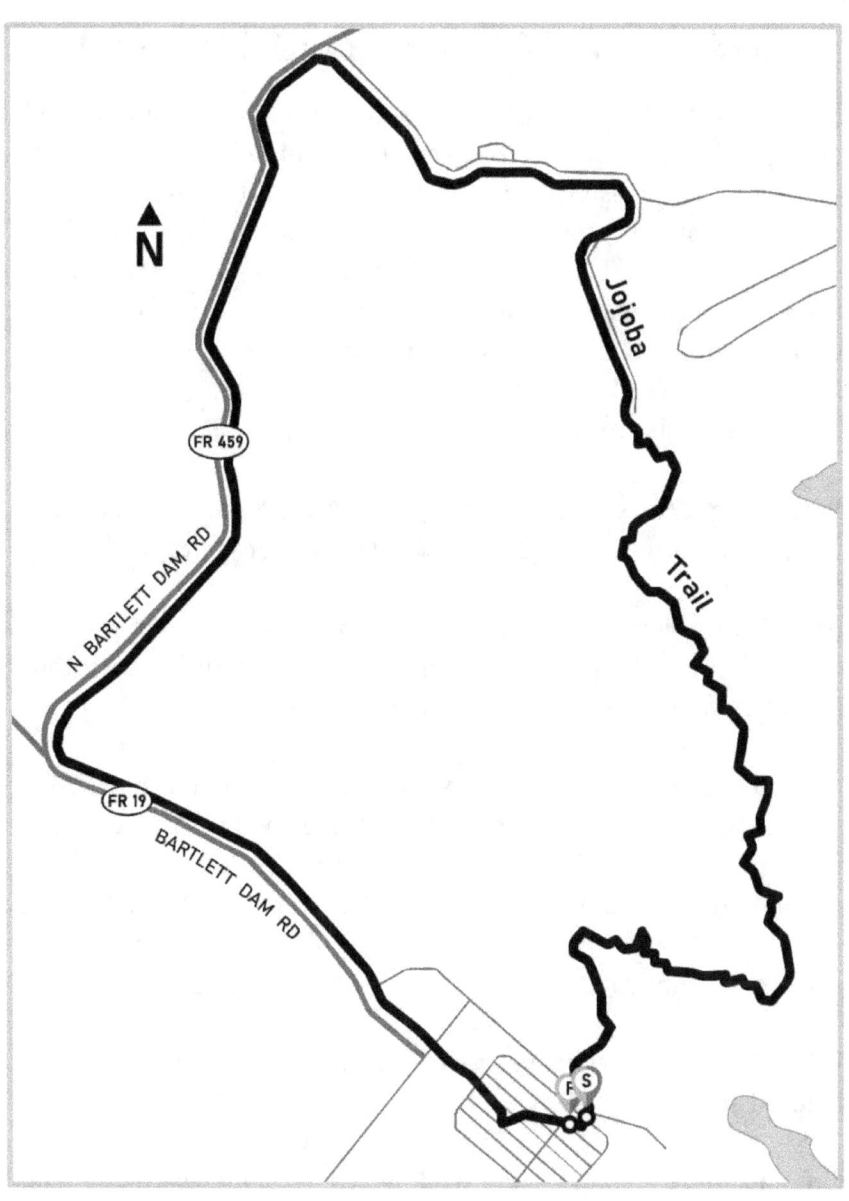

ROADRUNNER TRAIL - LAKE PLEASANT

Lake Pleasant Regional Park offers camping, hiking, swimming, scuba diving, fishing, boating, horseback riding, and simply enjoying the beautiful Lake Pleasant surrounded by the desert landscape. A well-marked, easy (1) trail with constant views of the lake is the Roadrunner Trail. It is 1.6 miles total and features side trails down to the water. If the water is low, you can cross a small peninsula about 0.2 miles into the hike to a small indigenous ruin.

Best time to visit: Spring-fall

Pass/permit/fees: Entry fee is $7/day per car, $2/day for individual, $4/day per motorized vessel, and $2/day per non-motorized.

Amenities: Picnic areas including two ramadas along the trail, telescopes for stargazing, moonlight scorpion hunting guided tours, discovery center, restaurants, and a general store

How to get there: From Phoenix, AZ, head north on I-17 to SR74. Go west 10.8 miles to Castle Hot Springs Rd., then north 2.1 miles to Lake Pleasant Access Rd. Go 0.8 miles to South Park Rd. and turn right, continue 1.8 miles onto Overlook Rd., take a slight left North Overlook Rd., stay left on North Overlook Rd., and the Visitor Center will be ahead and slightly left.

What to pack: Swimsuits, towels, floaties/life preservers, picnic lunch, fishing gear

Can you find? Mule deer and wild burros, or donkeys, can be found around Lake Pleasant. In the spring, count the colors of all the beautiful desert wildflowers.

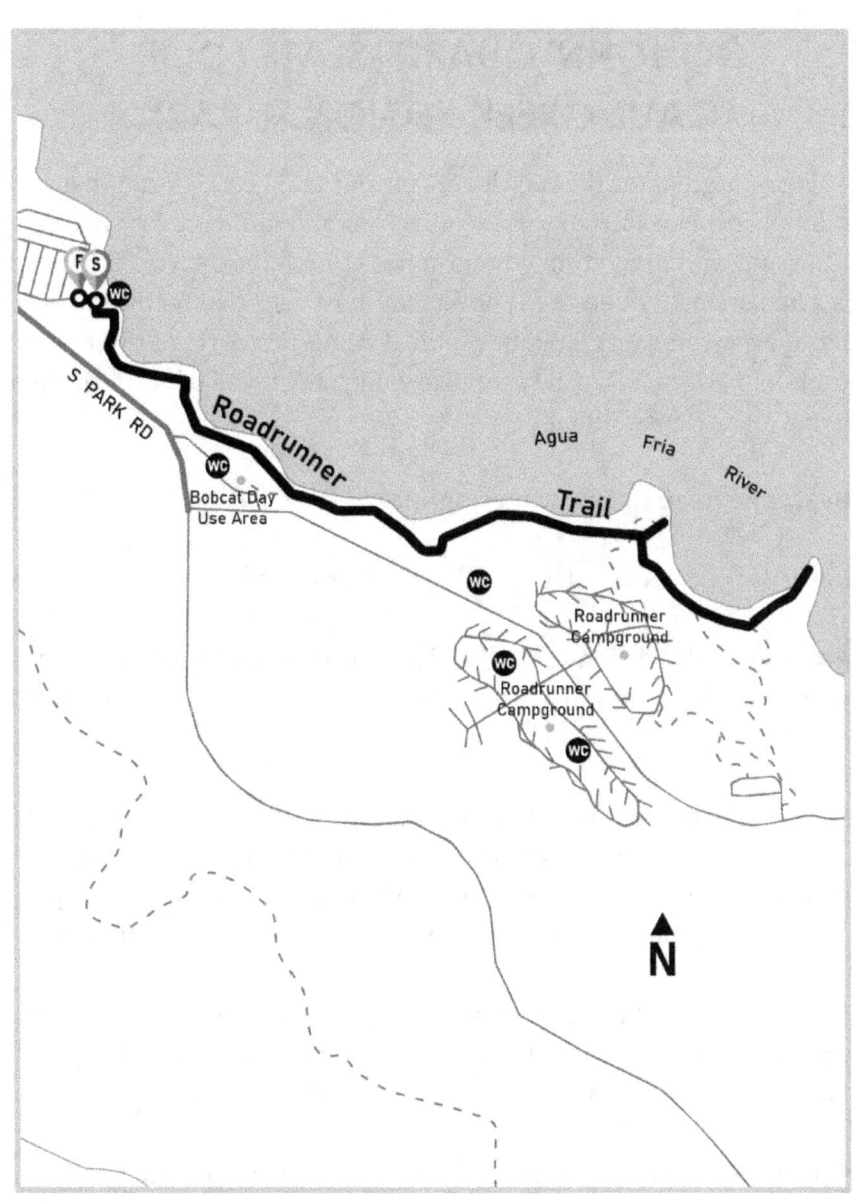

GO JOHN-QUARTZ-SLATE LOOP - CAVE CREEK REGIONAL PARK

This one is great for the rock lovers in your family! The location offers multiple trail options of varying distances and difficulty for whatever skills and ages are within your group. The Go John-Quartz-Slate Loop is a longer and moderate (3) option for most ages that features a little bit of everything. At 6.8 miles total, it combines parts of three great trails in the area. You can customize your route if you'd like to shorten it and make it less difficult.

Best time to visit: Fall, winter, spring

Pass/permit/fees: Entry fee is $7/day per vehicle.

Amenities: The park and trailhead have restrooms. The park also has ramadas, play areas, a store, a family campground, and a nature center.

How to get there: From Phoenix, AZ on I-17, take exit 223A/AZ-74 and head east towards Cave Creek. Continue 6.9 miles, then turn left onto North 32 St. Drive 1.8 miles to the entrance of the park. Go .75 miles and turn left on Tonalite Dr. for the Quartz Trailhead parking.

What to pack: There is no water access on the trail, so bring extra water. As there is no shade; bring sun protection. Snacks are great, too!

Can you find? Various rocks are found here, including slate and shiny white quartz. Look for fossils preserved in the slate and petrified wood.

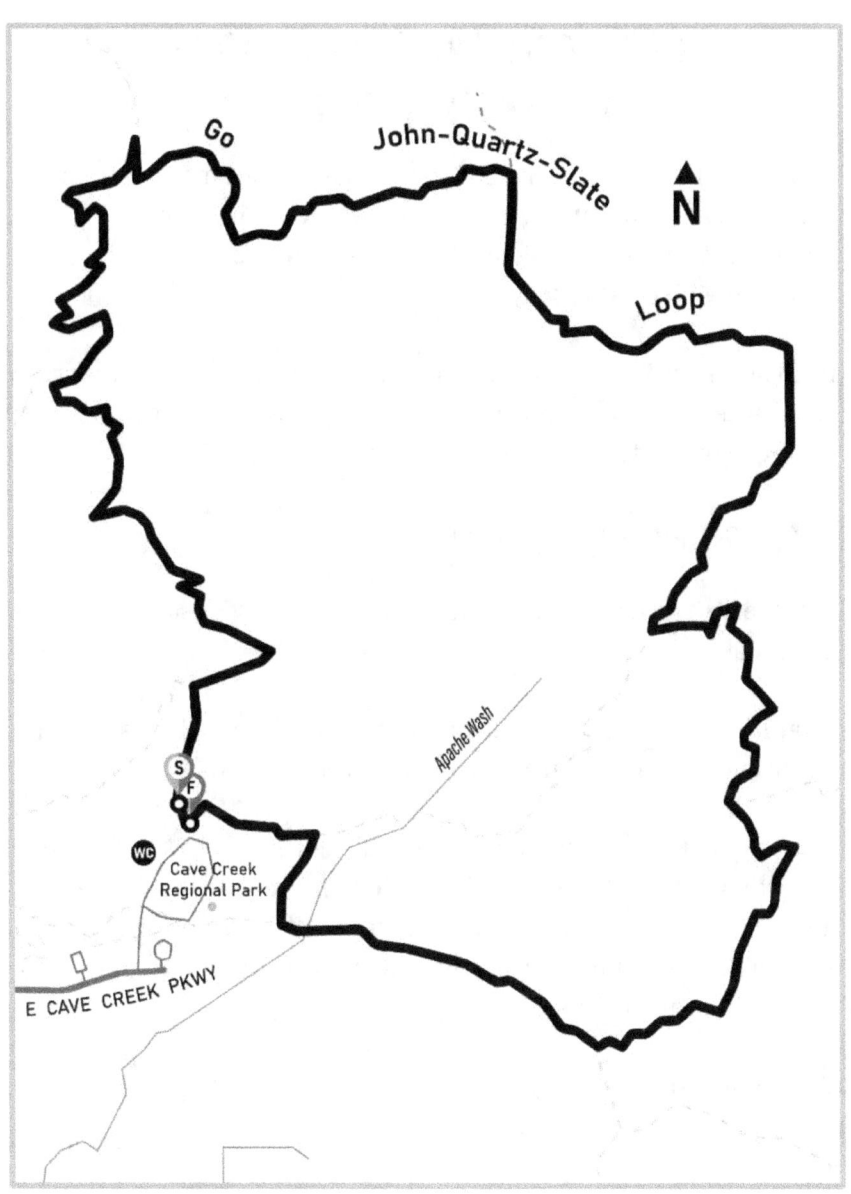

WHITE TANK WATERFALL TRAIL - WHITE TANK MOUNTAINS

Named for the white granite cliffs and "tinajas," or tanks/water pools, this trail terminates at a waterfall that flows if it has recently rained. Views of mountains and signs about local plant and animal life make it worth the hike either way.

At 1.8 miles, the trail is flat and easy (1), well-maintained, and partially paved. After the pavement ends, the trail is dirt/gravel with a staircase leading to the waterfall.

Best time to visit: November-April

Pass/permit/fees: The entry fee is $7/day per vehicle, $2/day per individual.

Amenities: Restrooms and drinking fountains near the parking lot, playground, and picnic area across the street

How to get there: From Phoenix, AZ, take I-10 west to the 101 Loop. Go north on 101 to Olive Blvd. Take a left and head west 13.5 miles to the White Tanks Park entrance. Continue on White Tank Mountain Rd. You will pass the information center at about 1.2 miles. Continue onto Waterfall Rd. and the parking lot.

What to pack: Hats, sunglasses, sunscreen, water, extra socks/shoes, extra clothes, binoculars, camera

Can you find? Don't forget to read about the wildlife of the area on the signs on the trail. You might also see some petroglyphs. Expect desert wildflowers and saguaro.

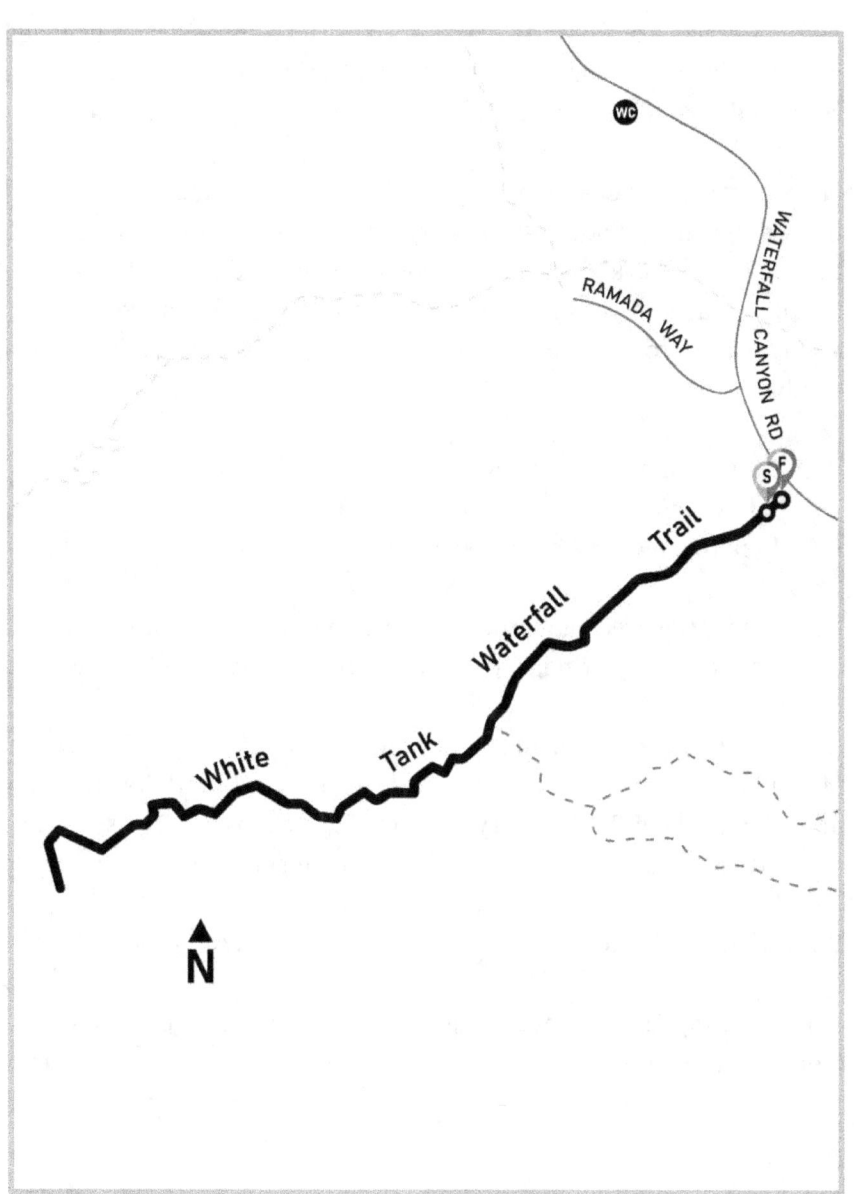

USERY MOUNTAIN REGIONAL PARK

There are hundreds of miles of trails to explore here. Park ranger-led desert education walks are also available. Let's focus on two recommended hikes for families, the Merkle, and the Vista Trails.

Merkle Trail is a super easy (1), flat loop of 1 mile that goes around the Merkle Hills. Vista Trail is a half-mile one-way trail that leads to the top of the Merkle Hills. It has some incline and is rated moderate (2-3), and at the top are views of distant mountain ranges. If your family is up to extending the adventure, the two trails can be combined.

Best time to visit: October-April

Pass/permit/fees: $7 entry fee into the park

Amenities: Covered playgrounds in the park, picnic tables, benches along the trail for resting, bathrooms on the northside of Merkle Loop

How to get there: From Mesa, AZ, take the AZ-202 Loop to Exit 24 for McKellips Rd. Stay on this road after the traffic circle and then turn left onto N. Ellsworth Rd./N Usery Pass Rd. Turn right onto E. Usery Pass Rd. Turn right to stay on Usery Park Rd. to Merkle Trail.

What to pack: Water, sunscreen, hats, sunglasses, camera

Can you find? Aside from the regular wildflowers and desert saguaro, look for cholla, mesquite trees, and palo verde.

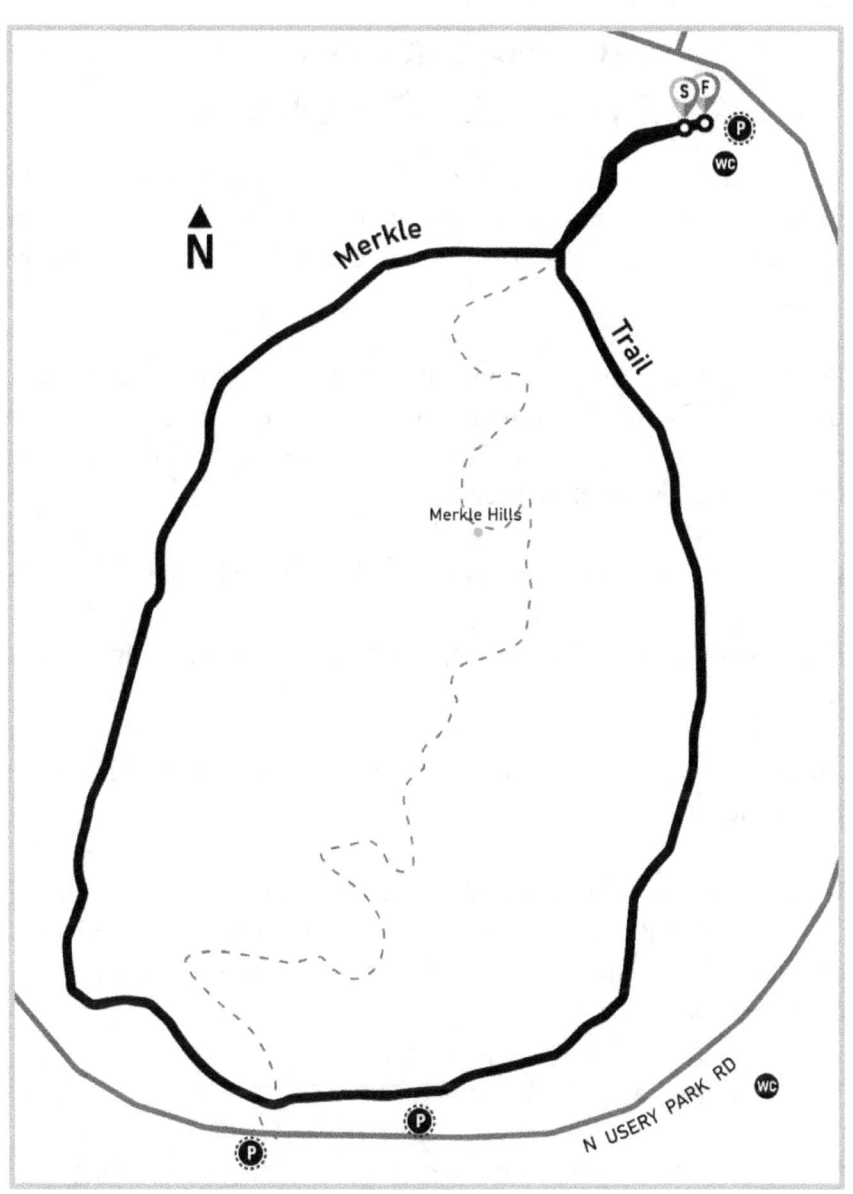

KACHINA HIKING TRAIL - SAN FRANCISCO MOUNTAINS

The Flagstaff area is well-known to hikers who love summiting peaks because of the abundance of mountains. Luckily, there's an easier alternative in the same area that features an old-growth forest in place of lofty summits.

Full of big trees, scattered boulders, canyons, wildflowers, and ferns, the full hike is 10 miles round trip and rated moderate (3). You can always hike partway to keep it young kid-friendly but be aware that there are higher elevations here.

Best time to visit: May-November, fall for beautiful colors

Pass/permit/fees: Backcountry permits are required during the winter.

Amenities: The Snowbowl Ski Resort is located at the trailhead parking lot.

How to get there: From Flagstaff, AZ, go north on US Rte. 180 for 7 miles to Forest Rd. 516 (Snowbowl Rd.). Turn right onto FR 516 and continue 6.3 miles to the parking lot, on the right. The trailhead is at the far end of the lot.

What to pack: Jackets, picnic lunch, camera, binoculars

Can you find? Scope out the Kachina Mountain peaks and Humphrey's Peak in the distance. There's also a distinguishable lava cliff you'll notice has black rocks. Aspen trees and Douglas firs can also be found in the area, and you might see mule deer, elk, or porcupines.

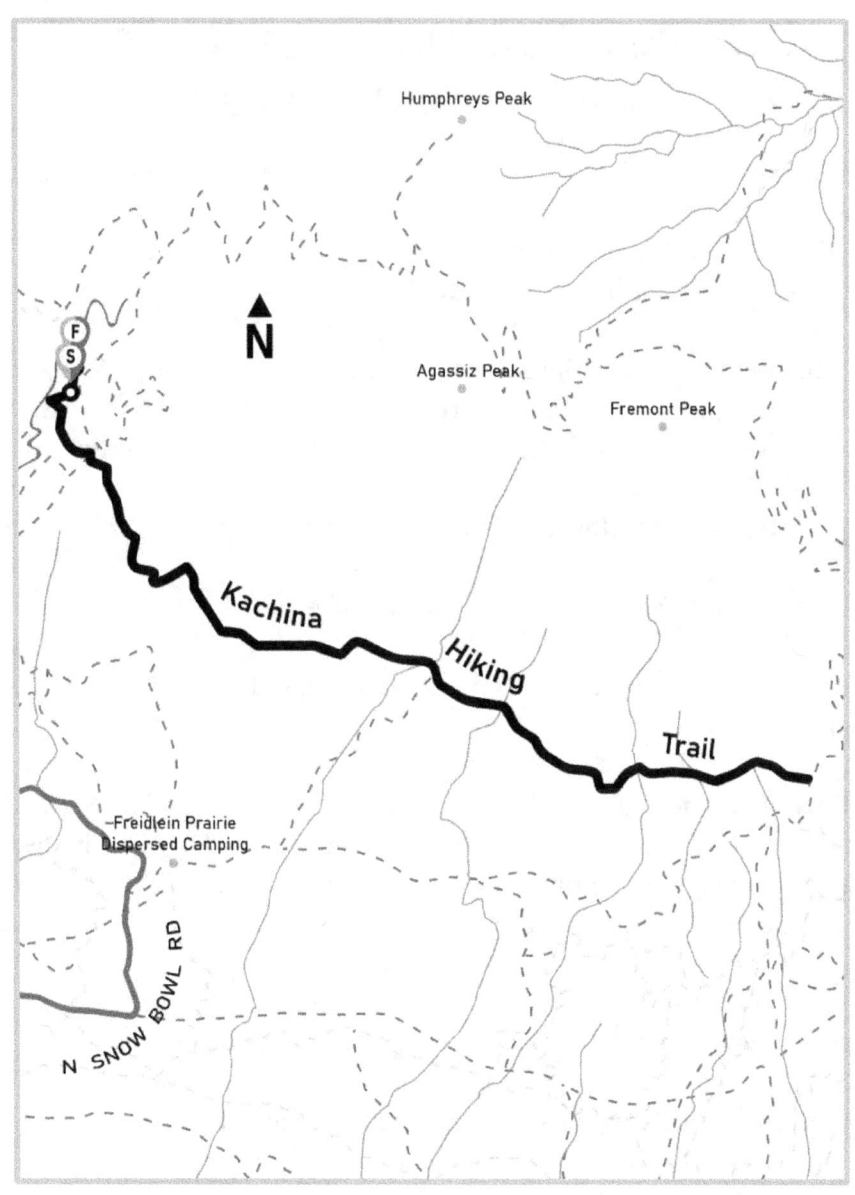

LOOKOUT MOUNTAIN TRAILS - PHOENIX MOUNTAIN PRESERVE

For a chance to hike to a peak of lower elevation, the Lookout Mountain Summit Trail is an accessible option. While it is a bit steep, it is a short trek and less traveled, too. At 0.9 mile out-and-back trail, the Summit Trail is rated moderate (3).

Families can also consider hiking around the mountain rather than up. The Lookout Mountain Circumference Trail is a 2.2-mile loop trail that is rated easy-moderate (2) and also offers great views and a river.

Best time to visit: November-April

Pass/permit/fees: No pass, permit, or fee required

Amenities: Bathrooms, drinking fountains, and playground at the park

How to get there: From Phoenix, AZ, take I-17 N/US-60 W to exit 211 for Greenway Rd. Merge onto N Black Canyon Acc and keep right onto W. Greenway Rd. Continue for about 4 miles and turn right onto N 16th St. Dr. until you see parking for the trailhead.

What to pack: It's rocky, so wear sturdy shoes. There's not much shade, so bring sun protection. A camera is always a great idea!

Can you find? The preserve is home to jackrabbits and desert cottontails. The Harris's Antelope squirrel is also common, whose bushy tail is held above its body like a parasol.

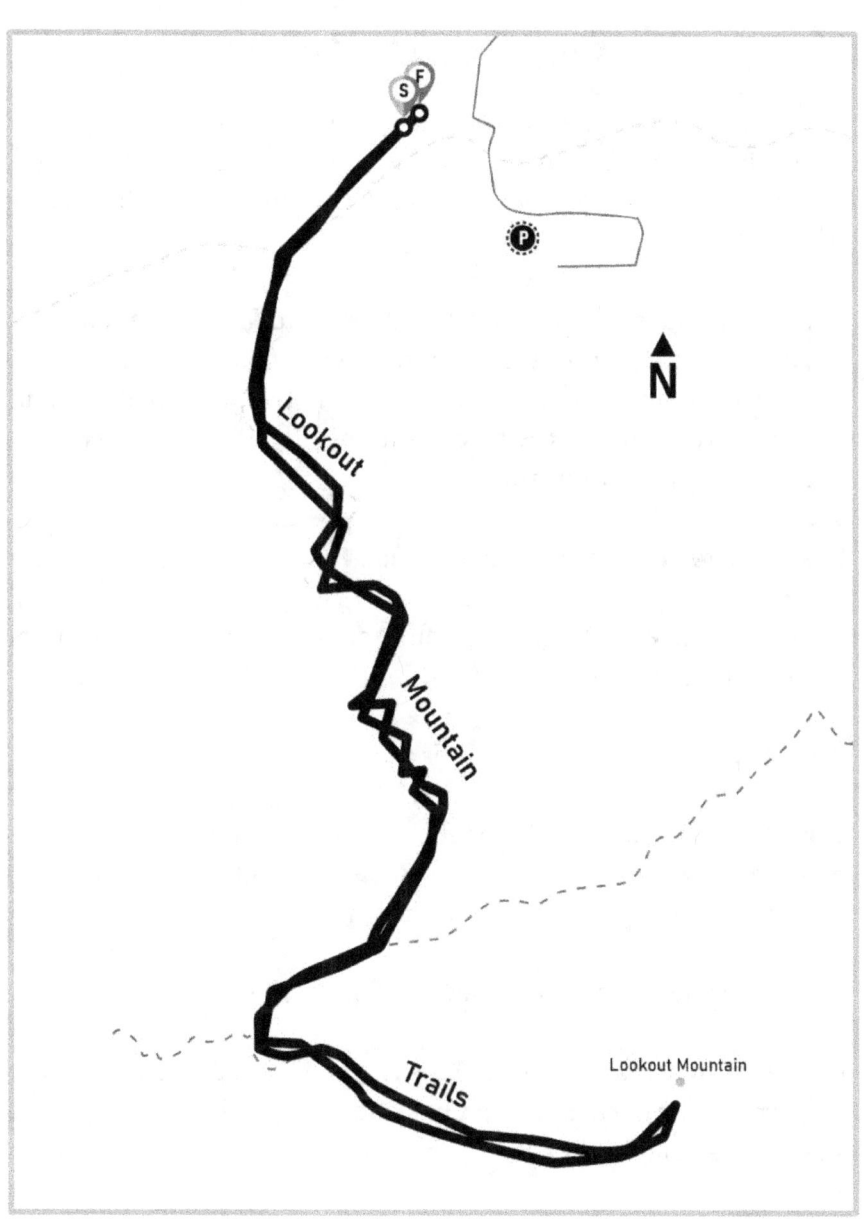

VEIT SPRINGS TRAIL

This picturesque alpine hike is loaded with history and lots to explore. At 1.7 miles, the loop is an easy hike that ventures near pioneer structures, such as a site with an old cabin built in 1892 by Ludwig Veit.

You can also take a short detour off the trail to find Native American pictographs and petroglyphs. A large plaque commemorating Lamar Haines, a Flagstaff conservationist, is an additional destination along the way. A rustic stone structure sheltering the spring is a nice feature to complete this short but eventful hike.

Best time to visit: Late spring-early fall

Pass/permit/fees: No pass, permit, or fee required. Backcountry permit required through mid-April.

Amenities: No restrooms or water access

How to get there: From Flagstaff, AZ, from the intersection of 180A and Snowbowl Rd., turn north onto Snowbowl and drive 4.2 miles. On the right side will be a turnout for the trail.

What to pack: Extra water, snacks, sun protection

Can you find? Read about the history of the area on Haines Plaque, and explore the ancient pictographs and petroglyphs. You might also see elk, deer, and wildflowers in the forest.

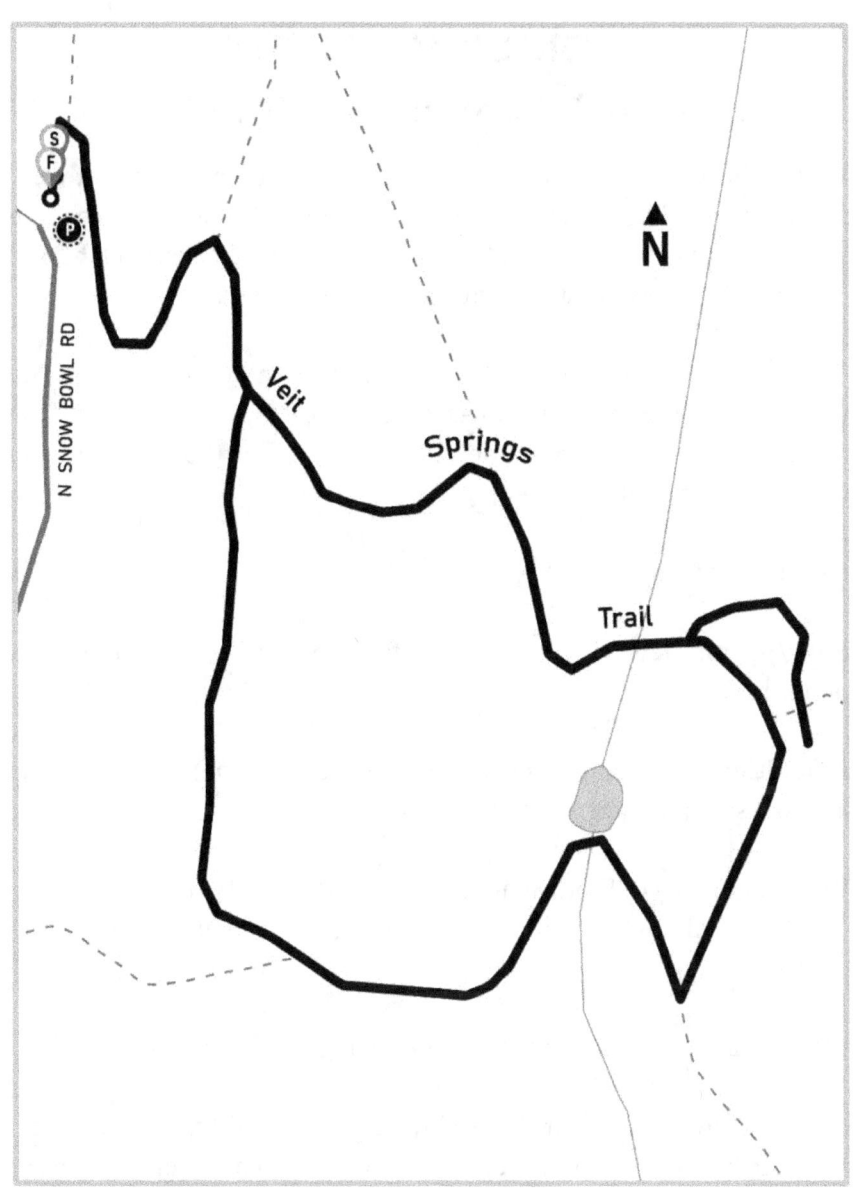

MONTEZUMA CASTLE NATIONAL MONUMENT TRAIL

Nestled into a tall limestone cliff sits a twenty-room, five-story, well-preserved dwelling that was built and occupied by the Sinagua people in approximately 1100-1425 AD. It's like an ancient, elaborate apartment complex that housed a village centuries ago.

The site is easy to access and is located near the visitor center. The paved trail is 0.33 miles and takes you to the castle and beyond to view the castle. You can't enter the cliff dwelling, but there are several viewpoints and wildlife to enjoy too.

Best time to visit: Fall or spring

Pass/permit/fees: $10/adult entry fee good for 7 days, kids 15 and under require no fee

Amenities: The visitors' center includes a museum; shaded picnic areas, restrooms, and a water refill station.

How to get there: From Sedona, AZ, take Hwy. 179 to I-17. Go south on I-17 to exit 289 east and follow the signs for about 3 miles to the entrance.

What to pack: Water, hats, sunscreen, sunglasses, picnic meal

Can you find? Watch out for prickly pear and cholla cacti. Tall yucca, creosote bushes, mesquite trees, desert willow, and Arizona sycamore are all trees to become familiar with. Rarely, you might encounter roadrunners.

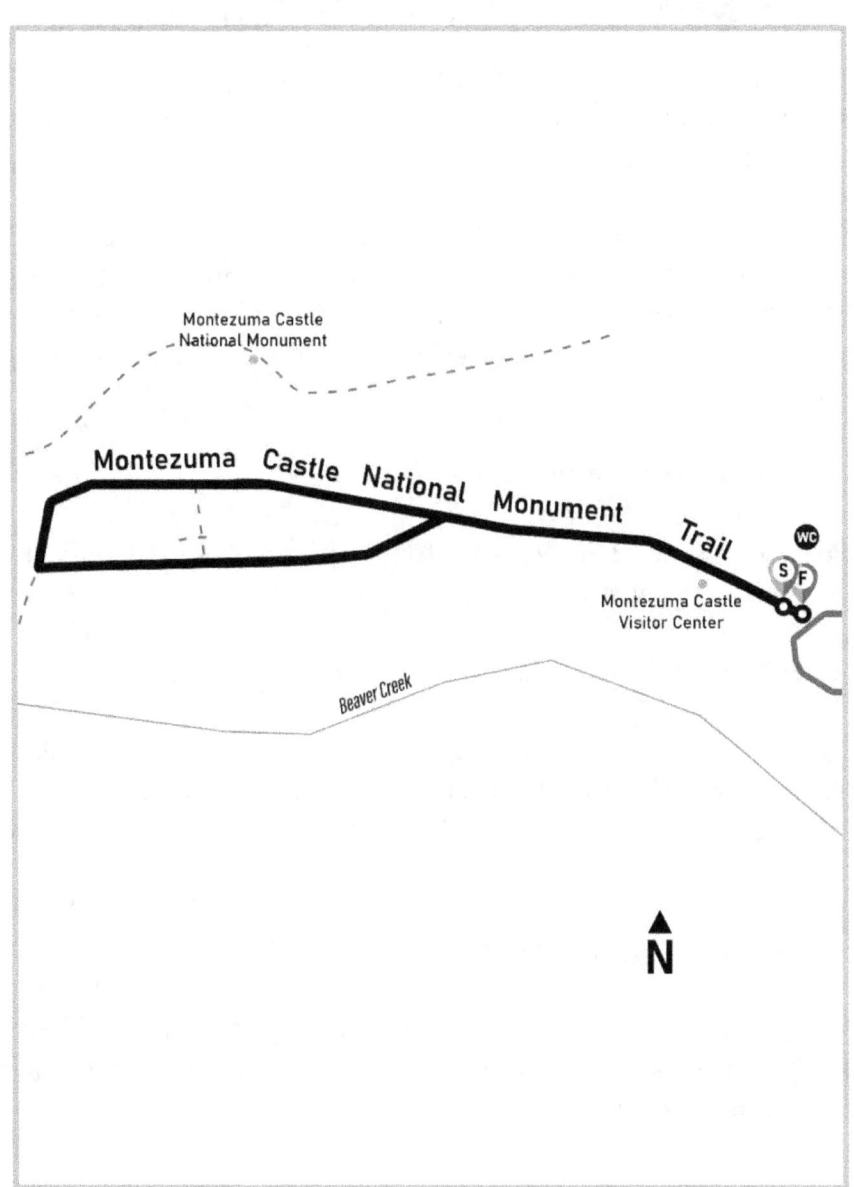

PINE & GOWAN HIKING TRAIL LOOP

Located along the Mogollon Rim, this trail is inside the Tonto Natural Bridge State Park. The trail is rated easy-moderate (2.5) with some steep, rocky portions, and is just shy of a mile total.

Pine-lined trails ascend to a 14-story natural bridge in this combined trail loop. It is the world's largest natural Travertine Bridge, and hikers might get misted from the waterfall dripping into the cavern. If you'd like to spend the day exploring, there are additional trail options.

Best time to visit: Spring or fall

Pass/permit/fees: Entry fee for Tonto Park - $7/adult, $4 per child 7-13. Children under 7 are free.

Amenities: Unsheltered picnic areas, restrooms in the park

How to get there: From Payson, AZ, go south on AZ-87 for 15.1 miles. Turn right onto Tonto National Forest Rd. 583 and continue downhill. Parking and trailheads are at the base of the hill.

What to pack: Bring water and extra clothes/socks/shoes. Wear sturdy shoes, as it gets slippery.

Can you find? It's always interesting to find lush moss in the desert. Rabbits, deep, or javelin may be seen running in the distance and beware of prickly pear cacti.

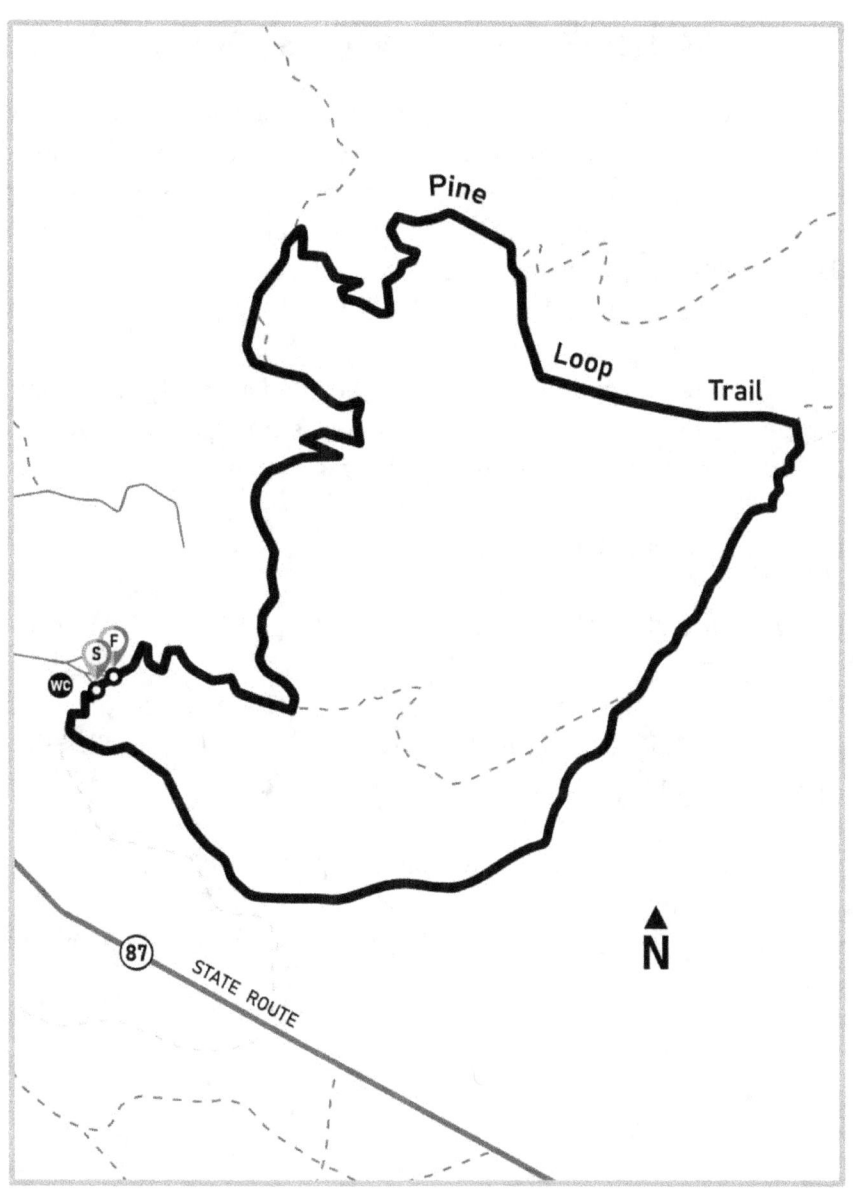

SOLDIER PASS TRAIL - SEDONA

The Soldier Pass Trail begins in an urban setting and travels into the Red Rock Secret Mountain Wilderness. Sedona is a favorite region of hikers, and this trail provides a cave, creek, arch, pools, wilderness, and a sinkhole. View the Devil's Kitchen Sinkhole and The Seven Sacred Pools formed among the desert backdrop. There's also Soldier Pass Cave and Soldier Arch.

This 4.5-mile out-and-back trail is rated moderate (3) with some climbing involved. There are additional trails throughout the area to extend your adventure. Note that parking is sparse in this area.

Best time to visit: Spring or fall

Pass/permits/fees: Red Rock Pass for parking - $5

How to get there: From Sedona, AZ, take Rte. 89A west to Soldier Pass Rd. Go right 1.5 miles to Rim Shadows Dr., then right 0.2 miles to a gated entry road to trailhead parking on the left.

What to pack: Water, sunscreen, hats, sunglasses, snacks, camera

Can you find? The Sedona Desert is home to mule deer, javelina, and desert wildflowers.

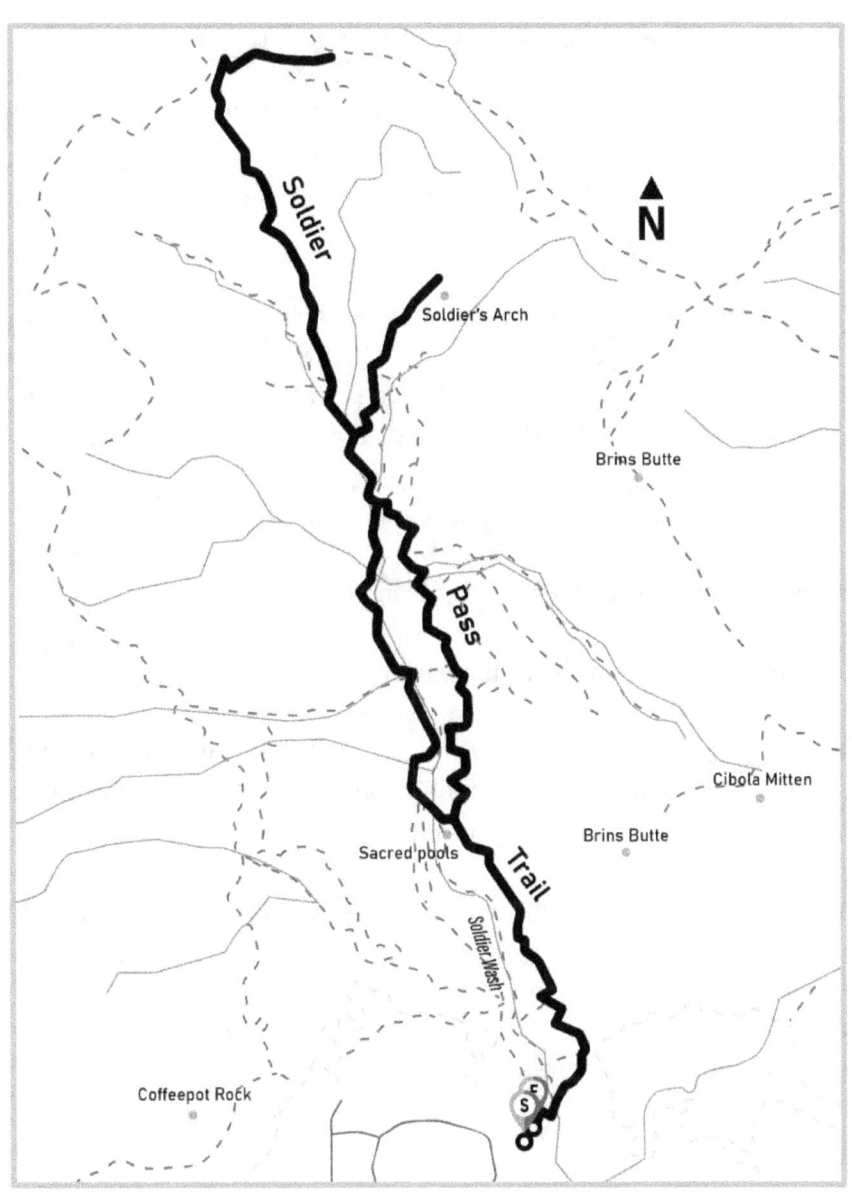

CATHEDRAL ROCK TRAIL

Cathedral Rock is a natural sandstone butte in the Sedona area which features spectacular views of the spires of red rock country. You can both hike around and up the Cathedral Rock, which is one of the most photographed sights in Arizona.

The 1-mile out-and-back trail is rated moderate (3), with some rock scrambling on an incline. You can hike up to the top of Cathedral Rock; however, this can be difficult and includes an elevation increase of 740 feet. Some points are nearly vertical climbs.

Best time to visit: Spring and fall on a dry day

Pass/permit/fees: Parking fee - $5 and very limited

Amenities: Restrooms near the parking area

How to get there: From the junction of Routes 89A and 179, take 179 south 3.5 miles to Back O' Beyond Rd. on the right. Go 0.6 miles to the trailhead parking turnout on the left.

What to pack: Sunscreen, hats sunglasses, water, camera, sturdy shoes, a backpack, trekking poles

Can you find? From the top of the trail, look out in the distance for signs of mule deer, coyotes, or javelina.

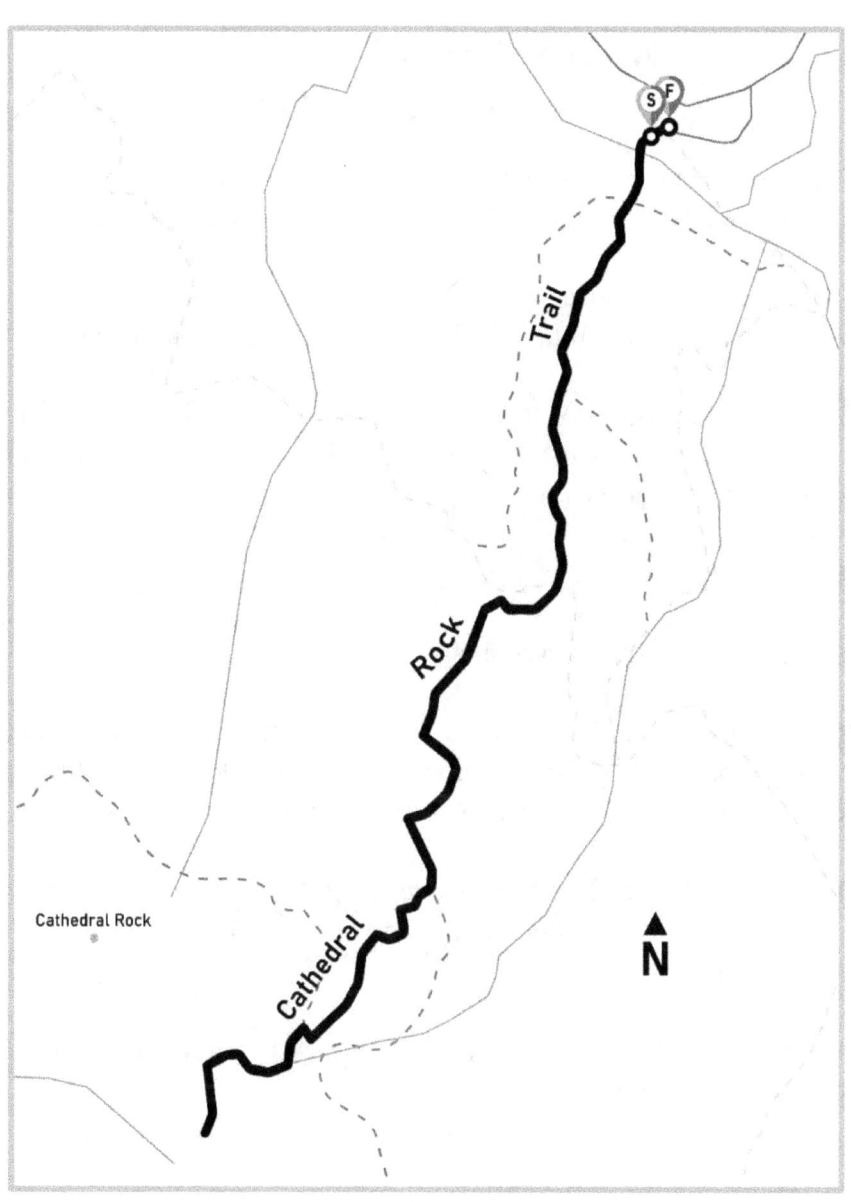

WATER WHEEL & ELLISON CREEK CASCADES

This very scenic hike features waterfalls and unique rock walls. The trail meanders along Ellison Creek, and there's a swimming hole.

The trail is short and easy, great for all ages, and rated easy (1). Out-and-back is 1.8 miles total, and note that the water is always cold.

Best time to visit: April-October; beware of flash flooding, especially during monsoon season (mid-June through September). Be certain to keep an eye on the weather.

Pass/permit/fees: $9 for parking

Amenities: Restrooms available

How to get there: From Payson, AZ, at the intersection of 87 A and 260, go north on 260 for 2 miles to Houston Mesa Rd. Turn right and continue 7.8 miles to the trailhead on the right.

What to pack: It can get slippery, so bring sturdy shoes and possibly trekking poles. Swimsuits, towels, and extra clothes/socks are also good options.

Can you find? There is a water wheel that was used to power an ore crusher in the 1930s.

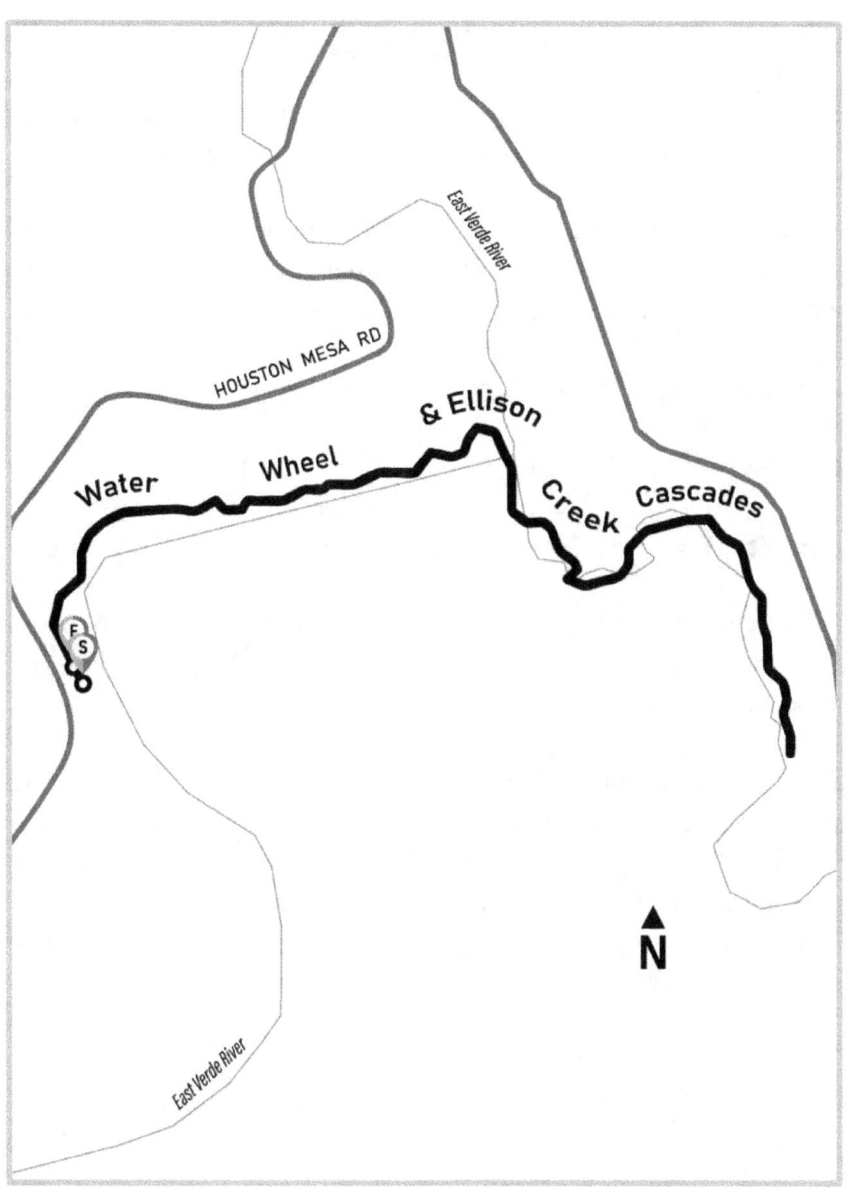

BADGER SPRINGS

Featuring the Agua Fria River and a high desert canyon, this hike offers easy terrain, shallow water, and swimming holes to enjoy.

The distance from the parking lot to the river is less than a mile and easy (1). There is a portion of the trail past the swimming holes that would make this a more moderate (2.5) hike.

Best time to visit: May or June

Pass/permit/fees: No fee

Amenities: No restrooms, some shade

How to get there: From Phoenix, AZ, take I-17 north to Exit 256 for Badger Springs. Follow the road about 1 mile to the parking area for the trailhead.

What to pack: Floaties, swimwear, water shoes, extra clothes/socks, sunscreen, towels, snacks, or lunch

Can you find?
Look for petroglyphs, crawfish, tadpoles, wildflowers, yucca, and/or creosote bushes.

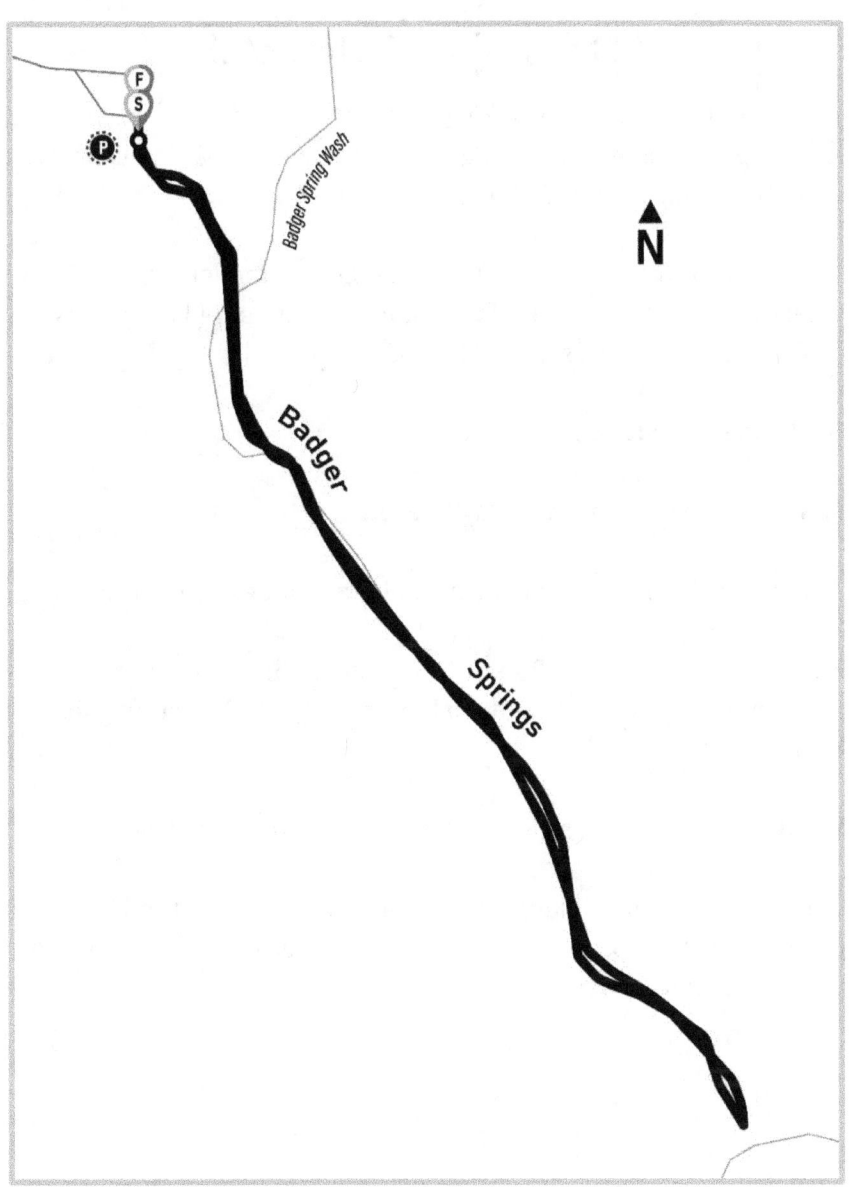

LYNX LAKE LOOP TRAIL

This man-made, 55-acre lake presents opportunities for boating, kayaking, canoeing, and fishing — but no swimming. The Loop Trail around the lake meanders through the forest as well.

There is a paved portion on the west side of the lake accessible to wheelchairs or strollers. This refreshing hike is easy (1), contains lots of shade, and measures 2.4 miles total.

Best time to visit: March-September

Pass/permit/fees: $5 cash day-use fee

Amenities: Restrooms and picnic tables are at Lynx Campground.

How to get there: From Prescott, AZ, take AZ-69 S to Walker Rd. Turn right and go 2.4 miles. Then turn left onto FR 24. The parking lot will be on your left.

What to pack: Water, snacks, sun protection, insect repellent

Can you find? While hiking near the lake, skim the cliffs and tree lines for bald eagles, osprey, waterfowl, and heron. Do you see any ponderosa pines?

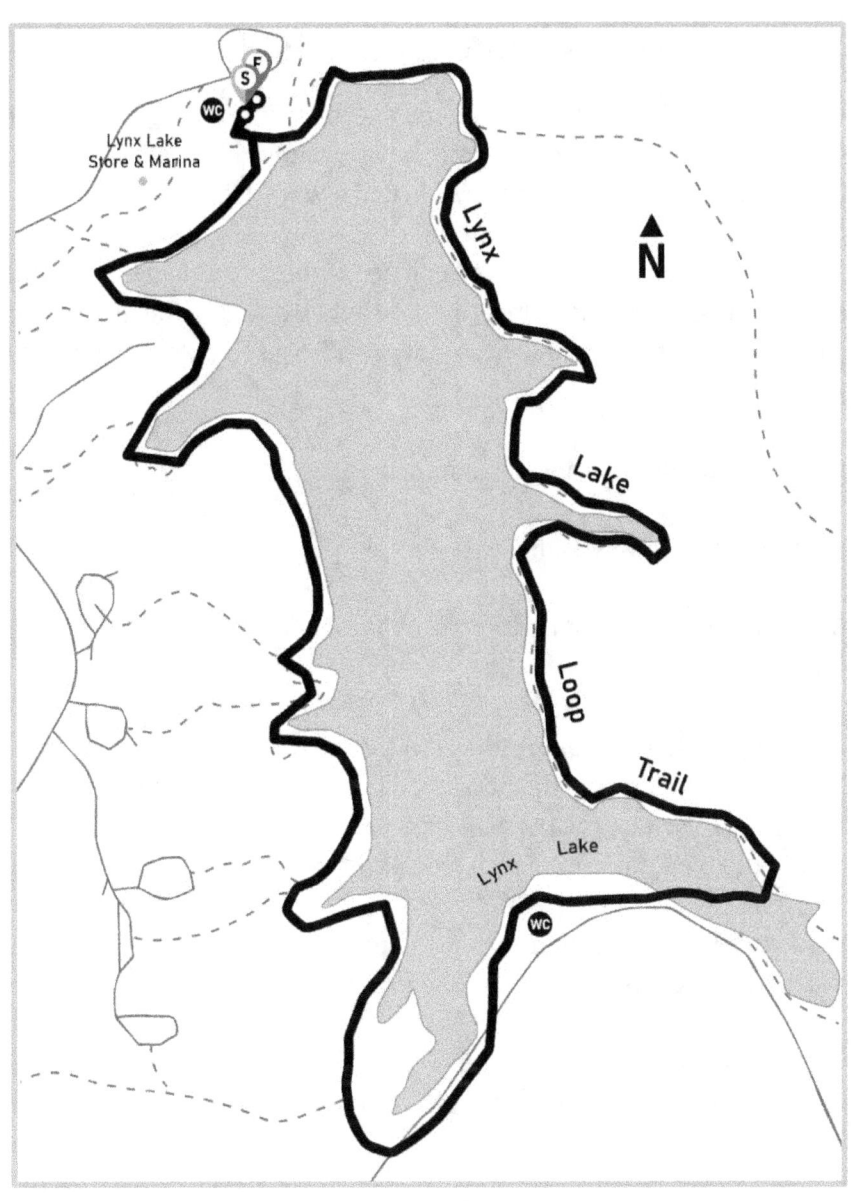

WATSON LAKE LOOP

Watson Lake is in the Granite Dells, which are cool granite rock formations that are smooth and have various interesting shapes. Nearby are also coves, rocky terrain, and a waterfall.

The loop contains multiple portions accessible from many trails you can link together. The entire loop is approximately 4.8 miles and includes easy through moderate options (1-3), so you can customize your hike.

Best time to visit: Spring and summer

Pass/permit/fees: $3 admission fee

Amenities: Picnic ramadas, restrooms, playground equipment, camping

How to get there: From Prescott, AZ, take AZ-89 N to Watson Park Lake Rd. After entering the park, turn left onto Hillsdale Rd. and park at the recreational area there. Access to the North Shore Hiking Trail is near the boat dock on the left side of the road.

What to pack: Water, sturdy shoes, insect repellent, sunscreen, hat, snacks, fishing gear

Can you find? The towering Granite Mountain can be seen in the distance. Also, check out the cattails around the lake.

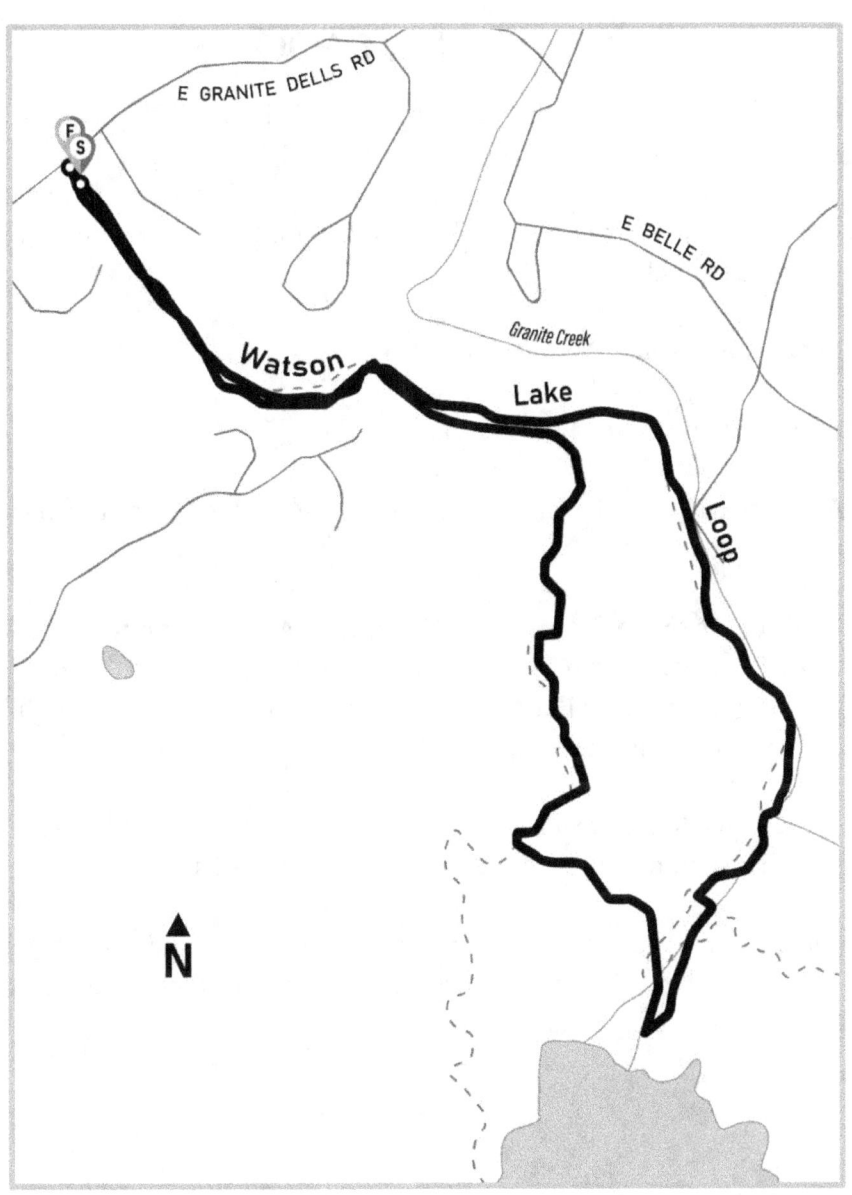

WILLOW LAKE LOOP

The trail is easy (1) on the western shore, where it's flat and grassy. The eastern shore is more moderate (2.5) and provides an opportunity for adventure and challenge, with boulders to climb, small canyons to explore, and views of the granite dells. The full trail is 5.2 miles total.

Best time to visit: March-October

Pass/permit/fees: $2 per vehicle

Amenities: Covered picnic areas, zoo at the entrance of the park, play area

How to get there: From Prescott, AZ, take AZ-69 North to AZ-89A Spur. Turn right and drive 14.7 miles to Willow Creek Rd. Turn left and drive 1.1 miles to Heritage Park Rd. and continue 0.2 miles to the parking lot for the trailhead.

What to pack: Bring sunscreen, a hat, sunglasses, water, and snacks. If it may be muddy after rain, bring extra shoes/socks.

Can you find? See Granite Mountain in the distance, and around the water, there may be waterfowl such as the Northern Pintail or Northern Shoveler.

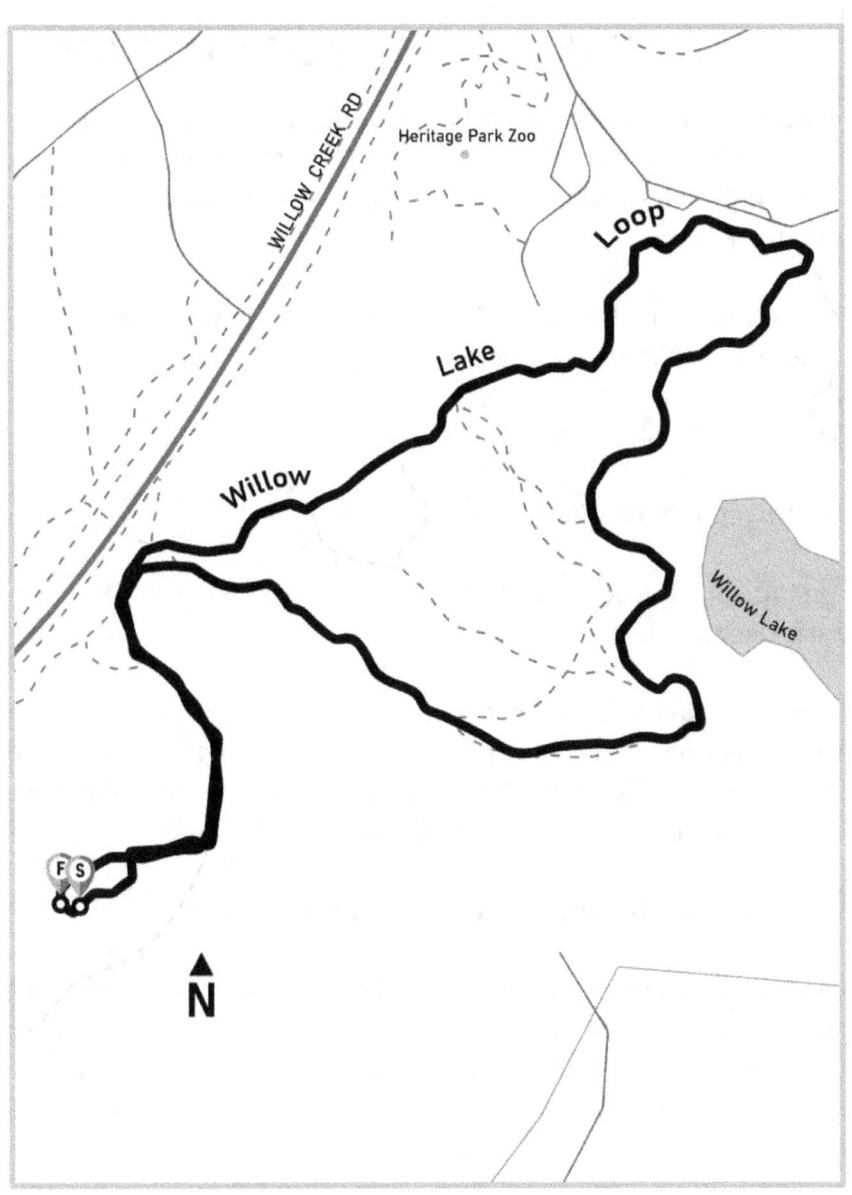

DEAD HORSE RANCH LAGOON LOOP

The Dead Horse Ranch State Park has multiple trails that are suitable for young kids and families. A popular trail system is the Lagoon Loop, which is 1.7 miles total and rated easy (1). There are three lagoons, each with its own loop.

The lagoons attract around 200 species of birds to watch. Biking and equestrian trails are in the park, too.

Best time to visit: Spring and fall

Pass/permit/fees: $7 per vehicle entry fee

Amenities: Restrooms at the lagoons, picnic areas throughout the park, camping sites

How to get there: From Cottonwood, AZ, head north on N 10th St. and follow the slight right toward Dead Horse Ranch Rd. Continue onto Dead Horse Ranch Rd. for 0.3 miles and follow it to the right in the park. Continue and the lagoons will be on the right.

What to pack: Fishing gear, bikes, sun protection, snacks/food

Can you find? The lagoons attract bald eagles, gray foxes, jackrabbits, and cottontail rabbits. Many species of fish live in the lagoons, such as the rainbow trout. If you're fortunate, you may come across river otters, too.

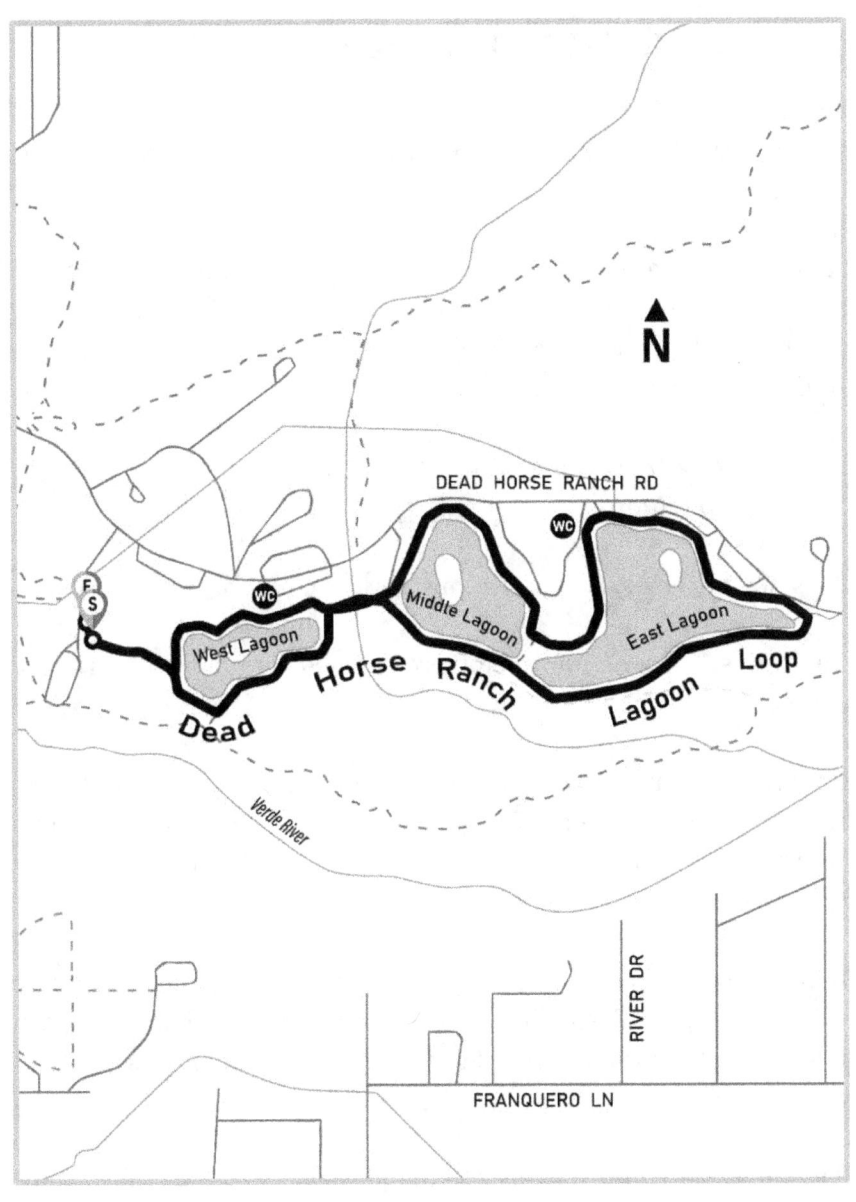

COCONINO LAVA RIVER CAVE

Located in the Coconino National Forest is a lava tube cave formed around 70,000 years ago. At 0.75 miles long, it is the longest of its kind in Arizona.

Some passages are over 30 feet tall, while others are only 3 feet, and the hike through is rated moderate (3). The temperature inside stays around 35-45 degrees Fahrenheit, so it's a great place to cool off in the summer months.

Best time to visit: Summer. Roads to the cave may be closed in snowy or muddy conditions.

Pass/permit/fees: No pass, permit, or fee required.

Amenities: There are no amenities on site, so use the restroom ahead of time.

How to get there: From Flagstaff, AZ, go north on US 180 for 9 miles and turn left on Forest Rd. 245. Continue for 1 mile and turn left onto Forest Rd. 171. Then turn left onto Forest Rd. 171B, which leads to the parking area.

What to pack: Warm clothes, jackets, sturdy shoes, at least three sources of light (flashlight/headlamp/glow sticks), helmet, water, snacks. The floor is uneven and gets slippery and there are some tight spots.

Can you find? Look up to see the unique lavacicles that appear to be dripping from the ceiling. Keep your eyes on the ground and walls and notice the volcanic rock ripples around you.

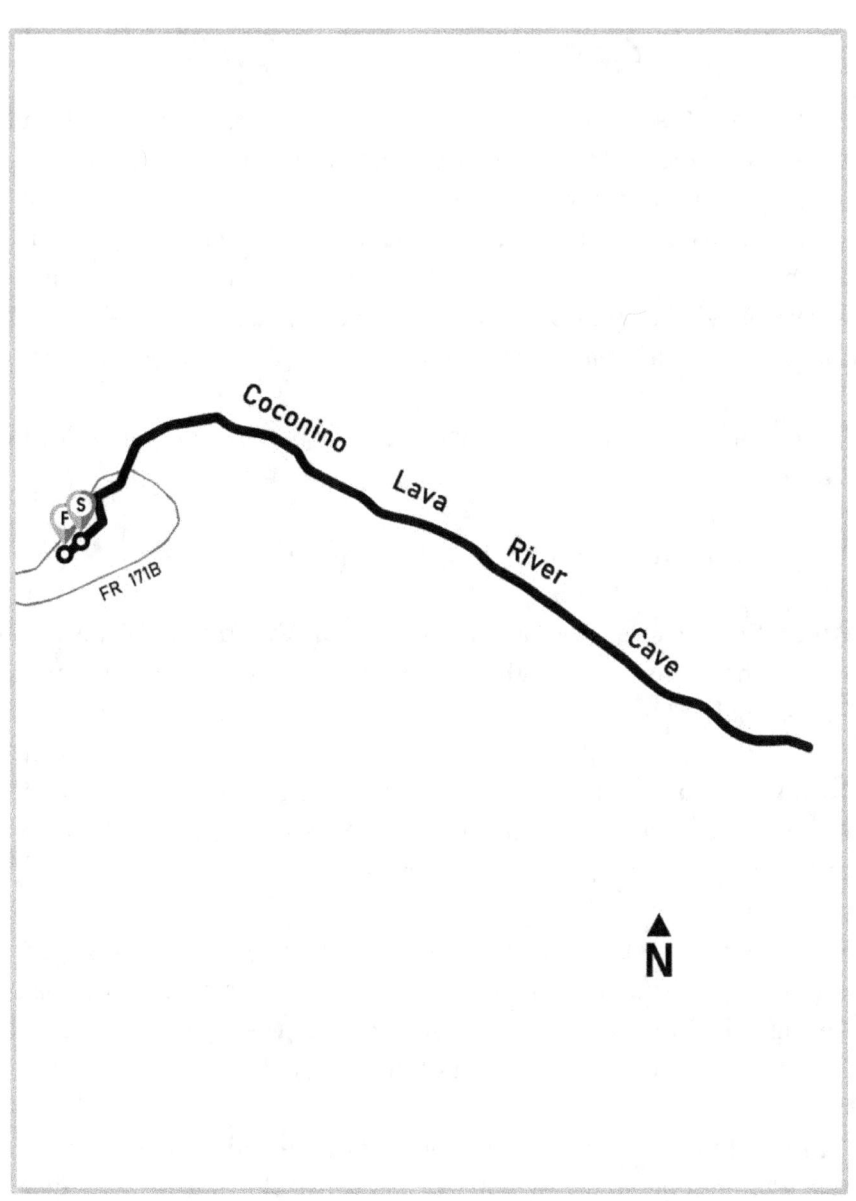

LYMAN LAKE STATE PARK

Lyman Lake State Park is full of prehistoric petroglyphs and ruins of the Hopi people, and there are three great trails accessible to kids. The shortest and easiest trail is the Peninsula Petroglyph Trail. At 0.25 mile and easy (1), it requires only a mild climb. The Ultimate Petroglyph Trail is half a mile and rated easy (2), but it is only accessible via boat/kayak/canoe. The Rattlesnake Point Pueblo Trail takes hikers to ancient ruins. The trail is easy (2) and only half a mile.

Best time to visit: Spring and fall. Summer is great for swimming in the lake.

Pass/permit/fees: $7 per vehicle day-use fee

Amenities: There are no restrooms on the trails. Water and restrooms are available at the visitors' center in the park. Camping is also available.

How to get there: From Saint Johns, AZ, head south on US-180 E/US-191 S/White Mountain Dr. toward E. 1st St. S. Continue for 11.9 miles and turn left at the Lyman Lake State Park entrance.

What to pack: Bring sun protection, snacks/food, fishing gear, camping gear, and binoculars. If you are planning to hike the Ultimate Petroglyph Trail, you may need your own kayak/canoe to access it because there are not always park tours available.

Can you find? Petroglyphs are abundant here and remember not to touch or step on any. The water draws great blue heron, mule deer, and elk to the area.

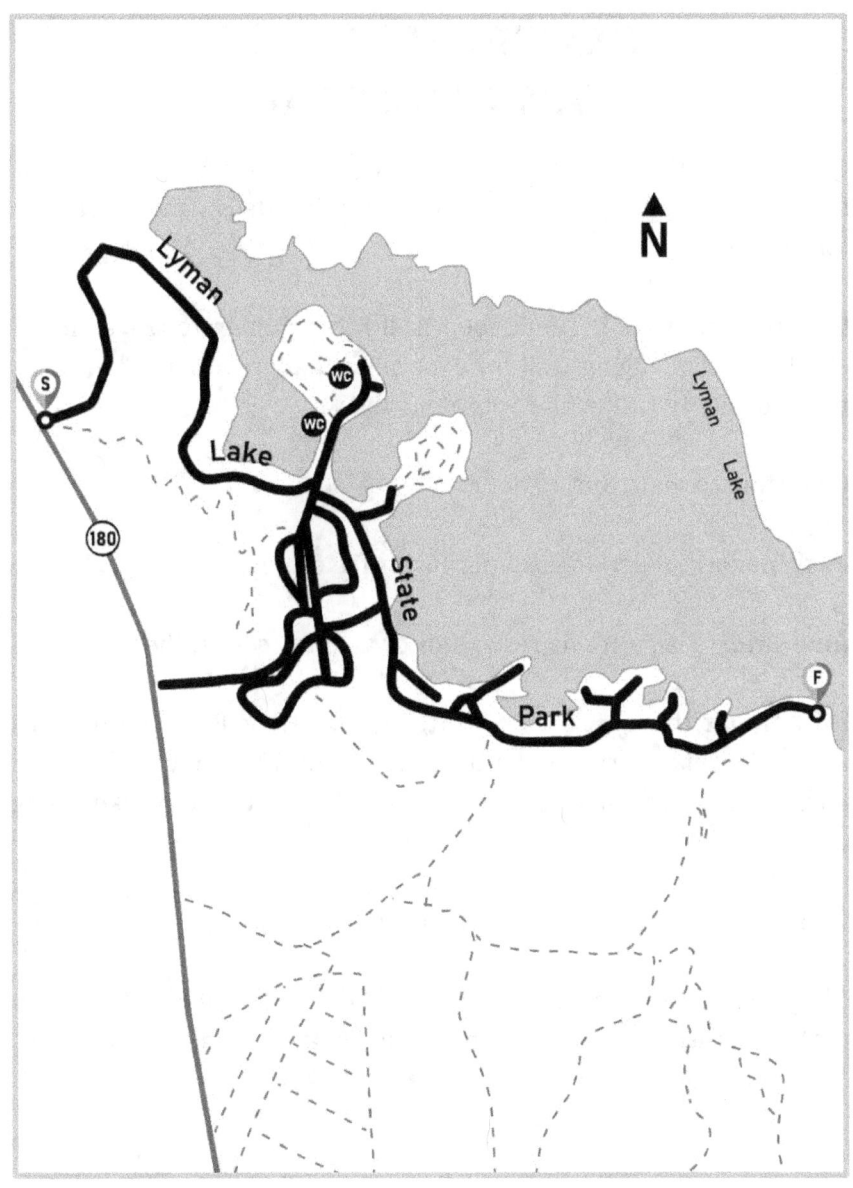

GRANITE GARDENS AT WATSON LAKE PARK

Overlooking Granite Creek in Watson Lake Park is a newer trail featuring a boulder tunnel, stairs, granite dells, and cool rock formations.

Granite Gardens is a 1-mile loop trail rated moderate (3), so it is a short and challenging trail for experienced adventurers. The trail is marked clearly with white dots along the way.

Best time to visit: Spring or fall

Pass/permit/fees: No pass, permit, or fee required.

Amenities: There are no restrooms or water access at the trailhead.

How to get there: From Prescott, AZ, take Hwy. 89 north past the lakes. There is a dirt road on the east side of the road called Granite Gardens Dr., just north of the High Rappel Area, that will take you to the trailhead.

What to pack: Sturdy shoes, sun protection

Can you find? Aside from the occasional fox or deer, look to the water for the hooded merganser, a small duck with a seemingly oversized, oblong head.

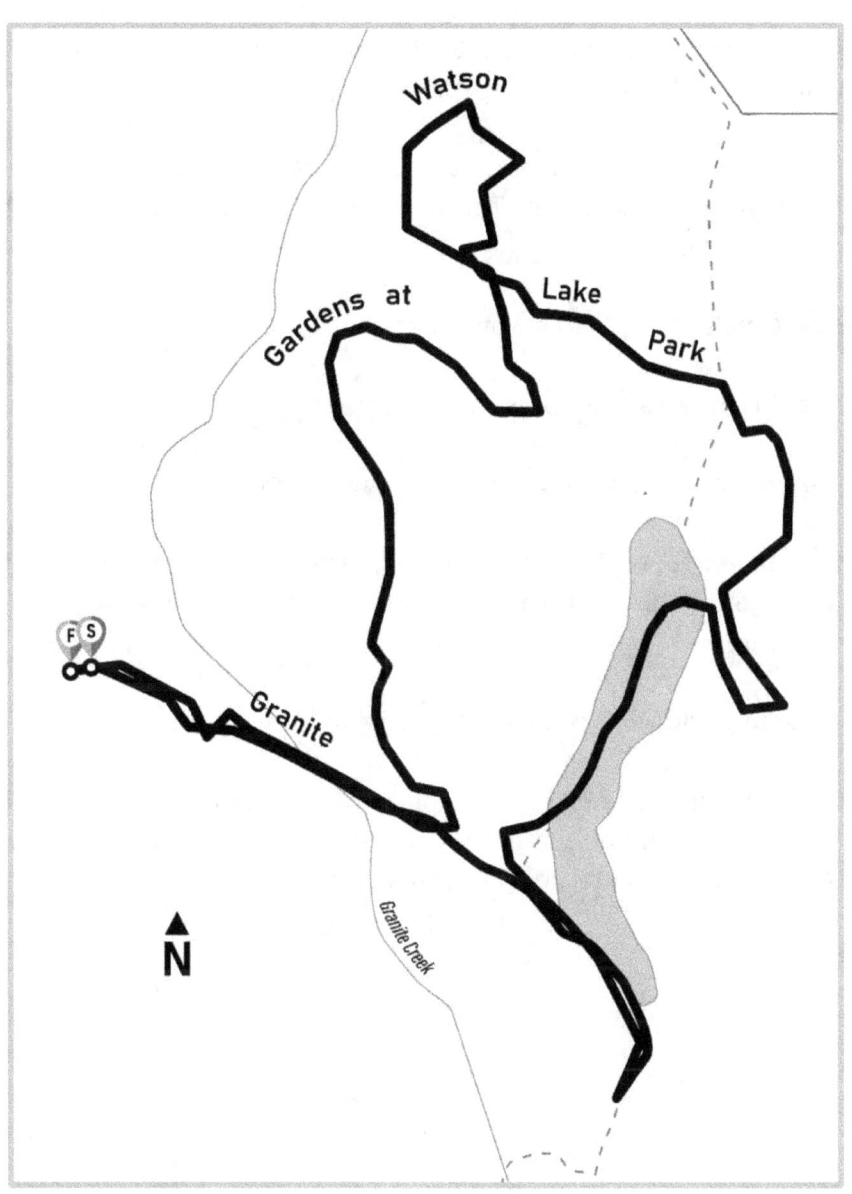

RED MOUNTAIN TRAIL

In Coconino National Forest is the Red Mountain Trail, featuring fantastic red rock formations. Red Mountain is a cinder cone volcano that rises 1,000 feet above the surrounding landscape.

The trail is 2.7 miles and rated easy (1). There is a short, sturdy ladder to climb up about 6 feet. The trail ends in an amphitheater that contains hoodoos.

Best time to visit: March-November

Pass/permit/fees: No pass, permit, or fee required.

Amenities: There are no restrooms or water access.

How to get there: From Flagstaff, AZ, take US-180 W/N Fort Valley Rd. to FS Rd. 9023V. Turn left and drive to the parking area for the trailhead.

What to pack: Extra water, sun protection, snacks

Can you find? At 12,633 feet, Humphreys Peak is the highest point of Arizona and can be seen from Red Rock Mountain. Along the trail, there are dark mineral crystals, junipers, and pines.

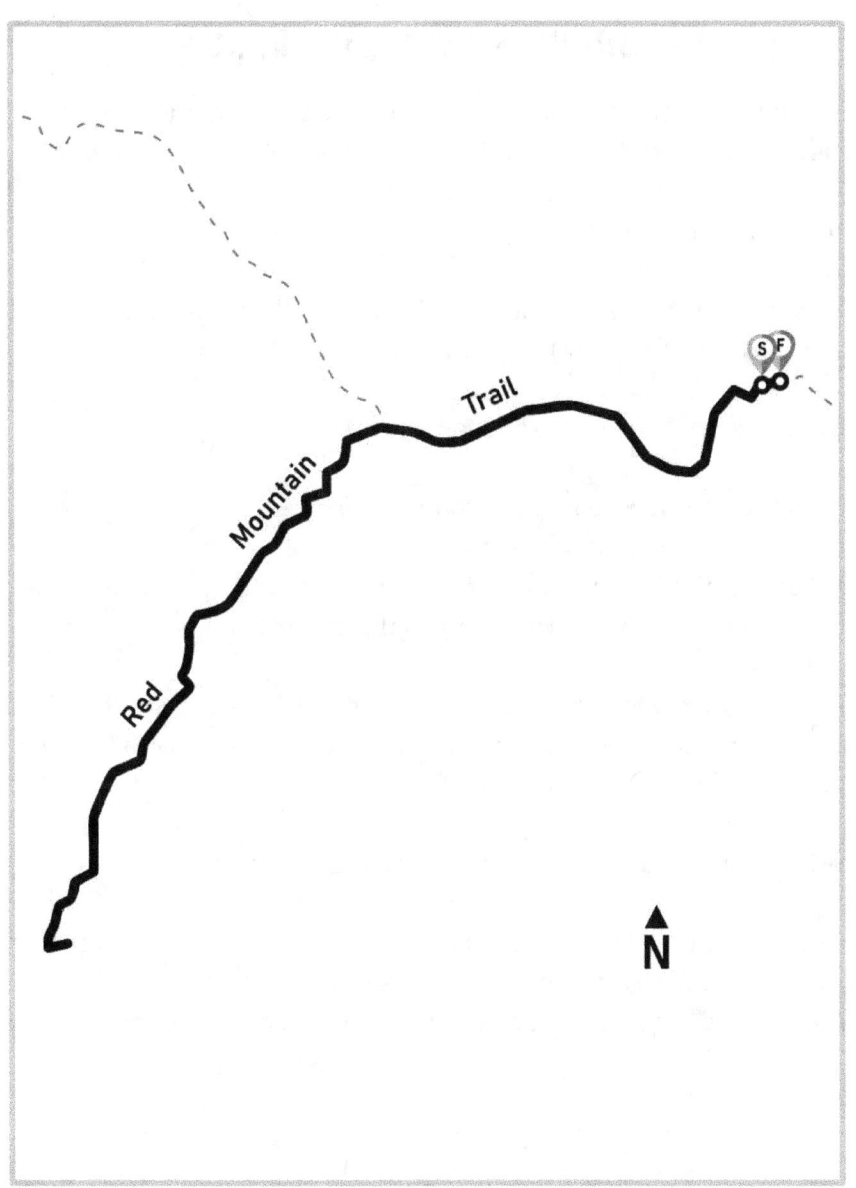

BROKEN ARROW TRAIL

The Broken Arrow Trail includes consistent elevation changes and various views, ending with a panoramic view of the Munds Mountain Wilderness. The Devil's Dining Room is a large sinkhole fenced off and seen early in the hike

This trail is rated easy (1) and is 3.5 miles total out and back. There is also a Jeep Trail nearby for off-roading.

Best time to visit: Spring and fall

Pass/permit/fees: $5 Daily Red Rock Pass

Amenities: There are no water or restrooms at the trailhead, so take care of these needs before driving to the parking area.

How to get there: From Sedona, AZ, drive on AZ-179 south. At the second traffic circle, take the third exit onto Morgan Rd. Go 0.6 miles to the trailhead parking on the left.

What to pack: Water, sun protection (depending on the time of year)

Can you find? The wide vistas offer views of many cactus varieties, such as king cup cactus, prickly pear, and yucca plants. There are also javelina and mule deer around, with a few cottonwood trees.

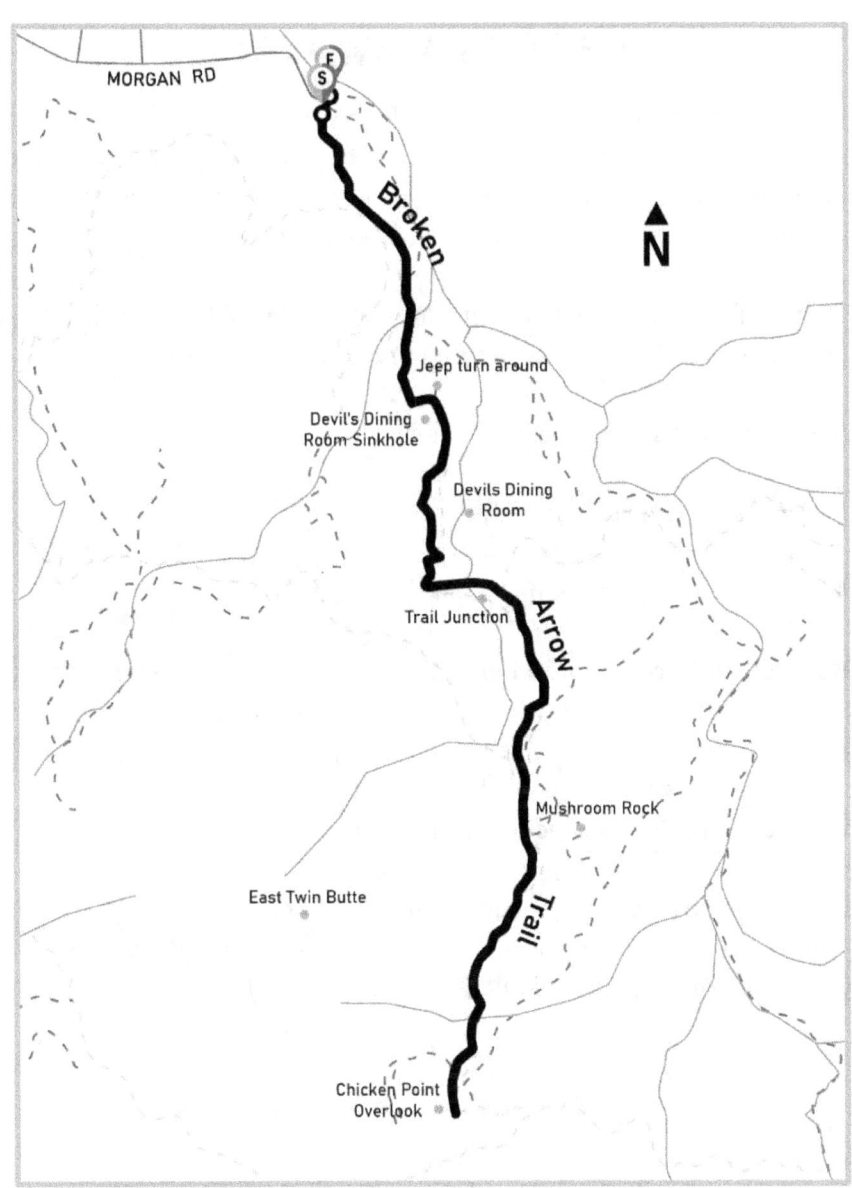

BELL ROCK PATHWAY TRAIL

Leading around the picturesque Bell Rock and Courthouse Butte rock formations, this trail offers great views the whole way. The Bell Rock Pathway Trail is 1 mile, flat, and easy (1). It is also stroller-friendly but is a bit gravely, so your stroller would need large wheels.

There's also a more challenging trail that climbs Bell Rock, called the Bell Rock Loop Trail, which is rated moderate (3).

Best time to visit: Spring or fall at sunset

Pass/permit/fees: $5 per day

Amenities: Vault restrooms on-site

How to get there: From Sedona, AZ, head south on AZ-179 S for about 30 miles. Watch for signs for Courthouse Vista and turn left for the parking area.

What to pack: Sun protection, water, snacks

Can you find? You might see quail or rabbits away from the trail. There have also been sightings of stag beetles. Around the trail, see if you can identify agave and yucca plants.

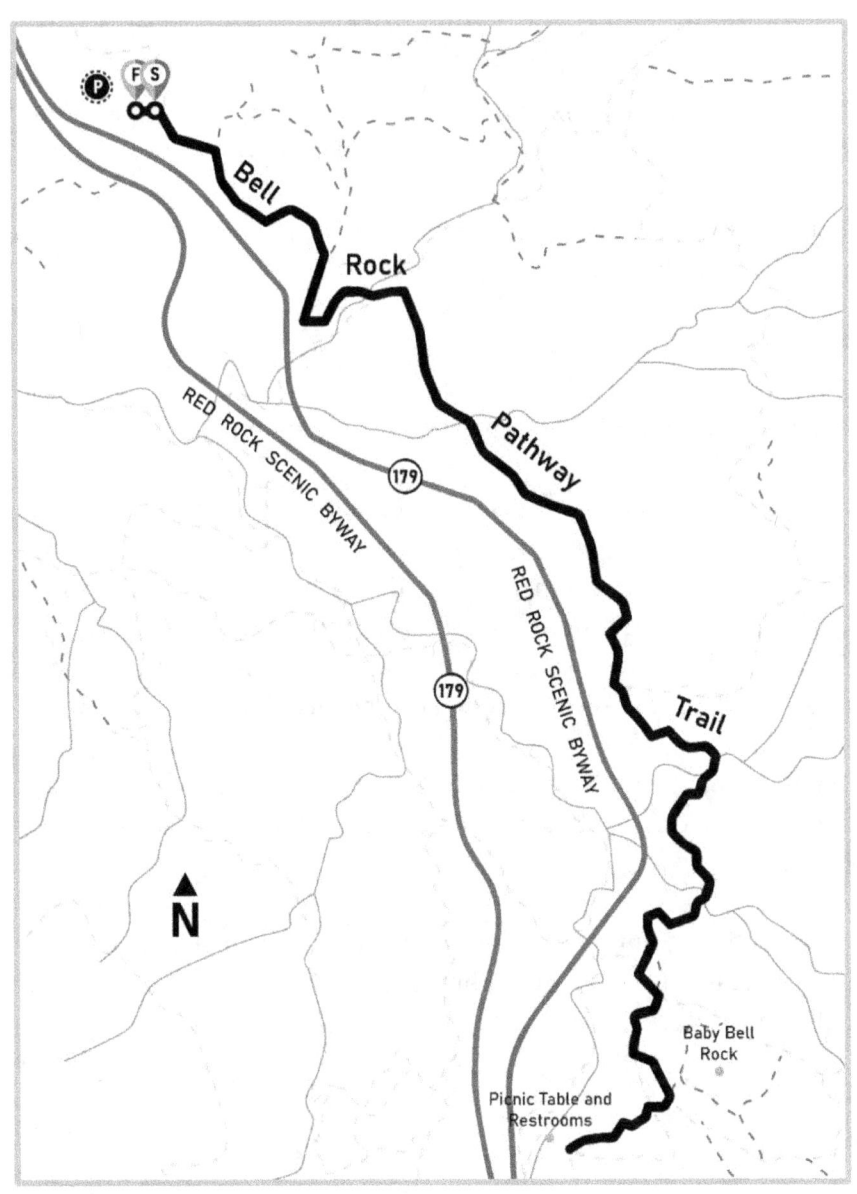

SEE SPRING TRAIL

This shady hike is a moss and fern oasis, where cascading springs and boulders abound, and leads to another hidden spring.

The trail is rated easy (2) and is 3 miles total. There is a creekside nook near the side of the trail to stop for a nice picnic.

Best time to visit: April-October

Pass/permit/fees: No pass, permit, or fee required

Amenities: Restrooms on-site, no drinking water access

How to get there: From Payson, AZ, head east on AZ-260 to the Christopher Creek Loop. Turn left and continue 1 mile to Forest Rd. 284. Turn left, and the trailhead will be 1.7 miles further. A high clearance vehicle is recommended for the dirt road.

What to pack: It might be muddy after rainfall, so bring extra shoes/socks/clothes. Bug repellent and a picnic lunch are also good ideas.

Can you find? Mint grows nearby, and you might smell it. This area is also home to mule deer, hummingbirds, the Mexican spotted owl, and cliff chipmunks.

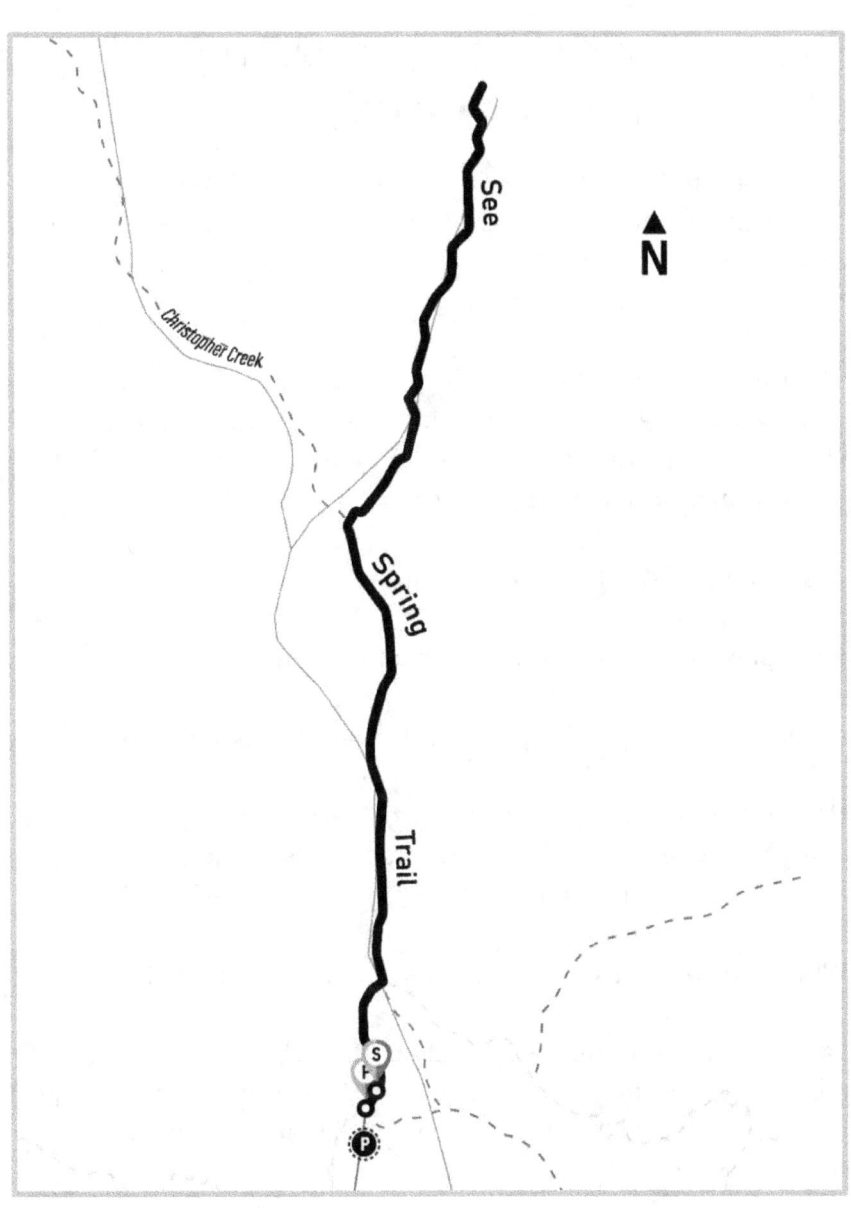

HAYDEN BUTTE PRESERVE & "A" MOUNTAIN

Hayden Butte Peak is better known locally as "A" Mountain for the giant whitewashed stone "A." The "A" was built by University of Arizona students in the early 1900s and is painted different colors depending on events and time of year.

There are parking lots toward the bottom and top for use depending on how much hiking you wish to do. The hike from the bottom is 1.7 miles total and rated easy (2). This is a great hike for college football fans and spectacular views of Tucson.

Best time to visit: November-February

Pass/permit/fees: No pass, permit, or fee required

Amenities: Stone gazebo, picnic tables. Restrooms unknown.

How to get there: In Tucson, AZ, take Congress St. west and turn left onto South Cuesta Ave. Continue onto Sentinel Peak Rd. S and drive for 1.6 miles. Continue until you see parking on the left.

What to pack: Trekking poles, water, snacks, sun protection

Can you find? The Sun Devils Stadium can be seen from a distance at the top of "A" Mountain. Also, read about the area on the informational plaques around the park. You may encounter petroglyphs on rock services around the mountain too.

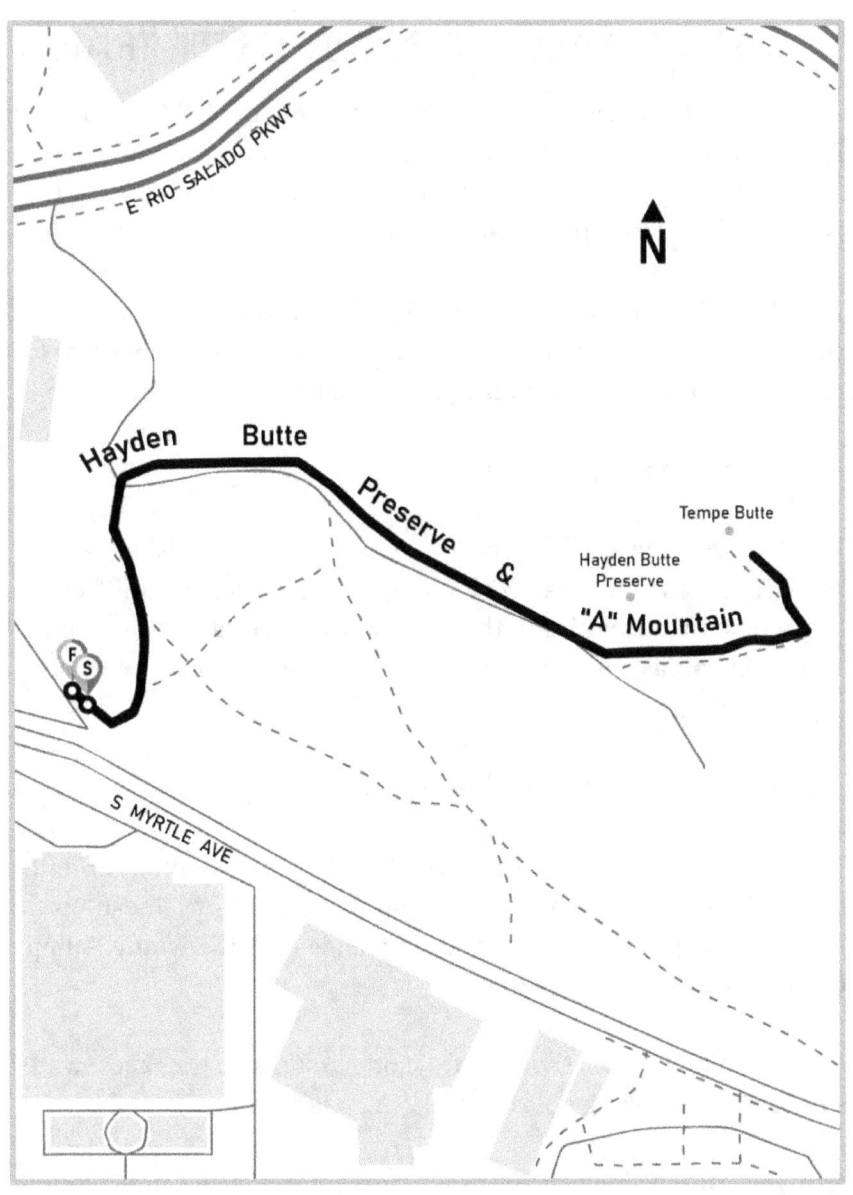

CIBECUE FALLS - CIBECUE CREEK TRAIL

A canyon adventure, this hike is located on the White Mountain Apache Reservation. It follows the Cibecue Creek, crossing back and forth, with some boulder scrambling. The waterfall is 30-feet-high and is a peaceful place with a small cave to rest in at the end of the trail.

The Cibecue Creek Trail is primitive and overgrown, so wear long sleeves and pants. It is 3 miles out and back and rated moderate (3). Also, take note that swimming is prohibited on Apache lands.

Best time to visit: Spring or fall

Pass/permit/fees: Permit required for all individuals, all ages. It costs $30/person per day. The "Cibecue Falls Access Permit" covers all recreational activities in the Cibecue Falls area and other general recreation areas on the reservation. Camping is available with a separate permit.

Amenities: Basic restrooms on-site, picnic tables

How to get there: From Globe, AZ, take US-60 East about 38 miles until Primitive Rd. Turn left and continue until the trailhead on the right. A high-profile vehicle is recommended for the windy, bumpy, dirt road and crossing the river.

What to pack: Water shoes, extra clothes/socks, extra shoes, water, sun protection, hiking poles

Can you find? Palo verde trees with green trunks and branches can be found around the creek. You might even spot an eagle among the cliffs.

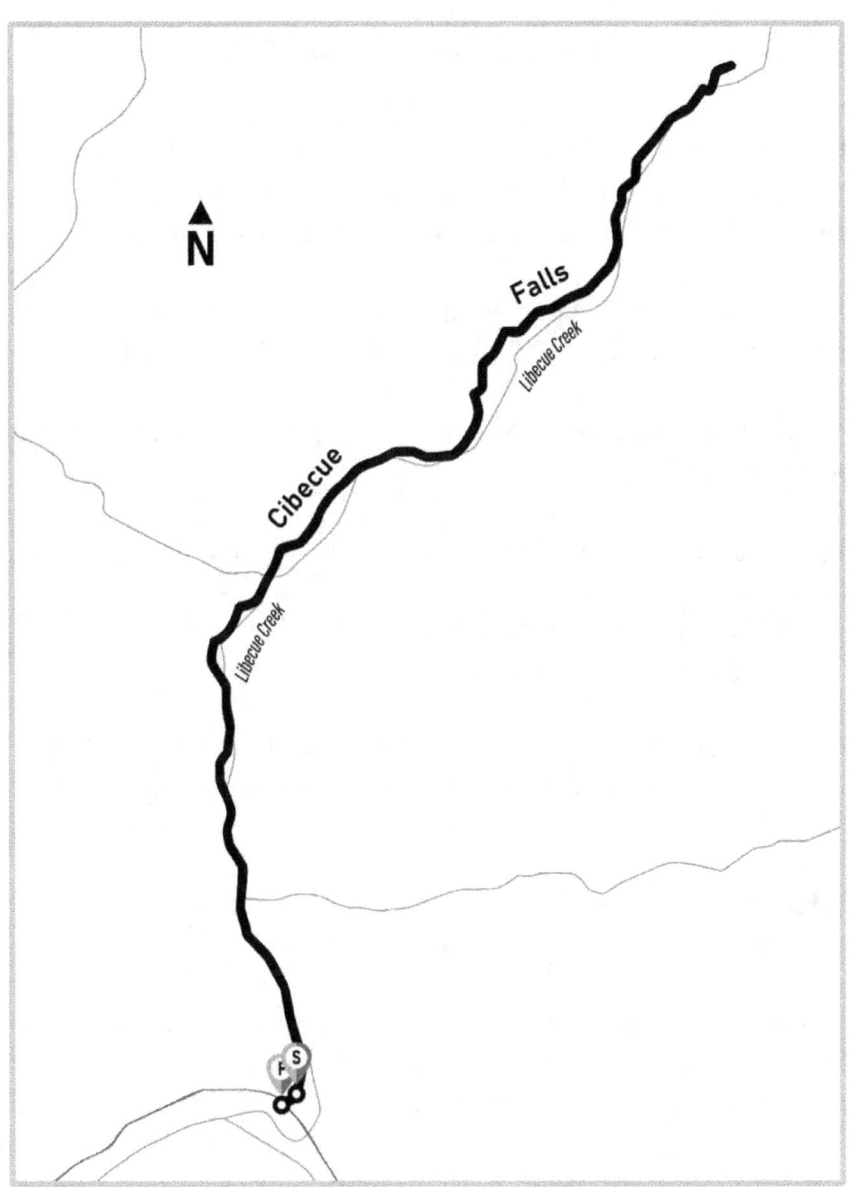

DEVIL'S BRIDGE TRAIL

The Devil's Bridge is a red rock arch that stands at 54 feet tall, 45 feet long, and 5 feet wide. From the parking lot of Devil's Bridge, it is 1 mile to the bridge or 2 miles total out-and-back, rated easy (2). There is some rock scrambling involved to get to the bridge.

A 4x4 vehicle is best for accessing this trail, but there is an alternate route that doubles the hiking distance from the Mescal Trailhead.

Best time to visit: Spring or fall. Start very early to avoid crowds at this popular site.

Pass/permit/fees: Red Rock Pass required - $5/day or $15/week

Amenities: There is a primitive restroom at the trailhead for Chuckwagon and Dry Creek Rd.

How to get there: From Sedona, AZ, get on AZ-89A south and drive to Dry Creek Rd. Turn right, and the parking area will be on the left in about 0.2 miles.

What to pack: There is very little shade, so bring sun protection along with snacks, a camera, water, and sturdy shoes.

Can you find? If you look closely at the rock formations, you might see balanced rocks or precarious boulders. Many species of wildflowers can be seen on the desert floor around you.

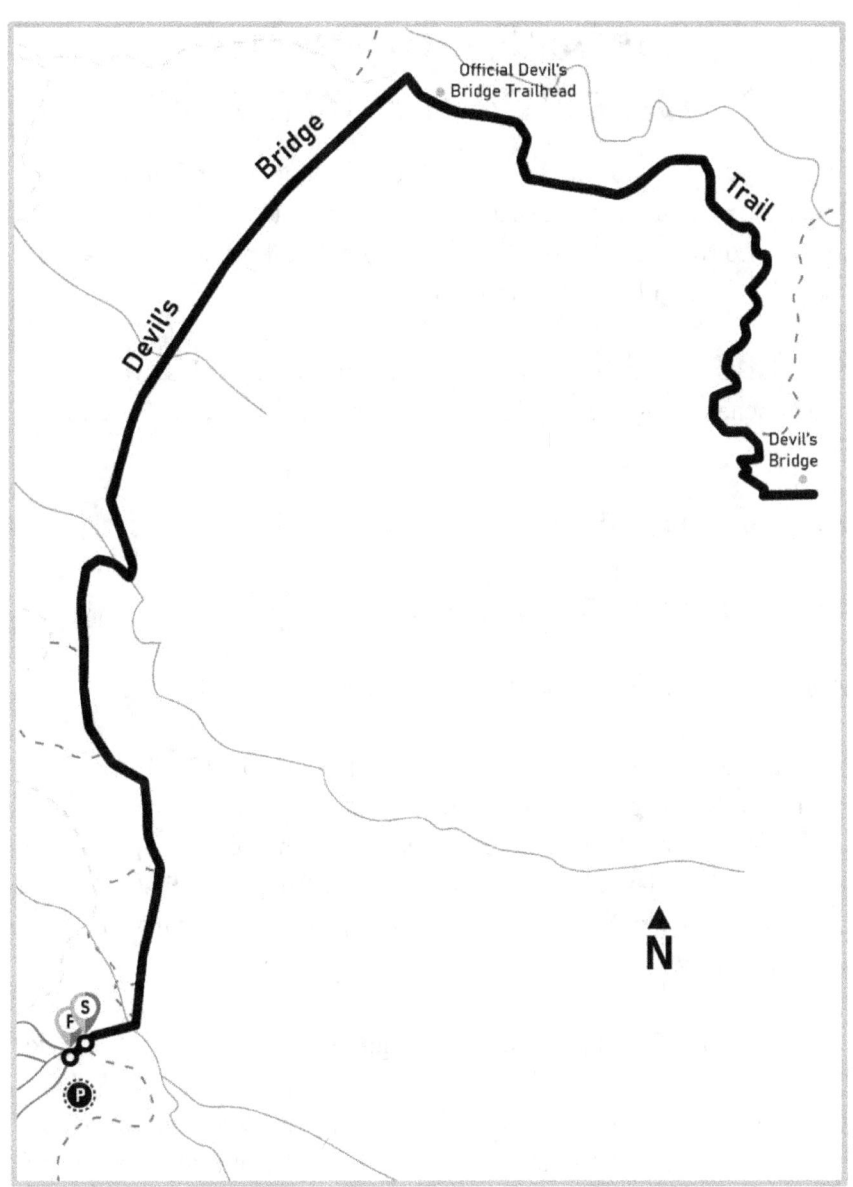

TREASURE LOOP TRAIL - LOST DUTCHMAN STATE PARK

Named for the gold mine rumored to have been found and then lost there, Treasure Loop features views of the Superstition Mountains and Tonto National Forest. The entire loop is 2.4 miles, rated easy (2), and hikes around rock formations.

The hike is extendable with Prospect's View and Jacob's Cross. There are benches along the way for breaks, making this trail very beginner-friendly.

Best time to visit: October-May

Pass/permit/fees: $ 10-day use fee

Amenities: Restroom on-site, picnic areas, water fountain

How to get there: From Phoenix, AZ, drive east on AZ-10 to exit 154 for US-60 E. Merge onto US-60 E towards Mesa/Globe and continue 24.6 miles to AZ-88. Turn left onto AZ-88, which becomes Apache Trail Rd. Drive 7.2 miles to the entrance of Lost Dutchman State Park, on the right. The trail is accessed from either the Saguaro or Cholla parking areas.

What to pack: Sun protection, trekking poles, camera, water, snacks

Can you find? Take in the view of the Superstition Mountains around you. Many cacti are found here, including the saguaro, ocotillo, and cholla. Other desert vegetation includes palo verde trees, mesquite bushes, and wildflowers.

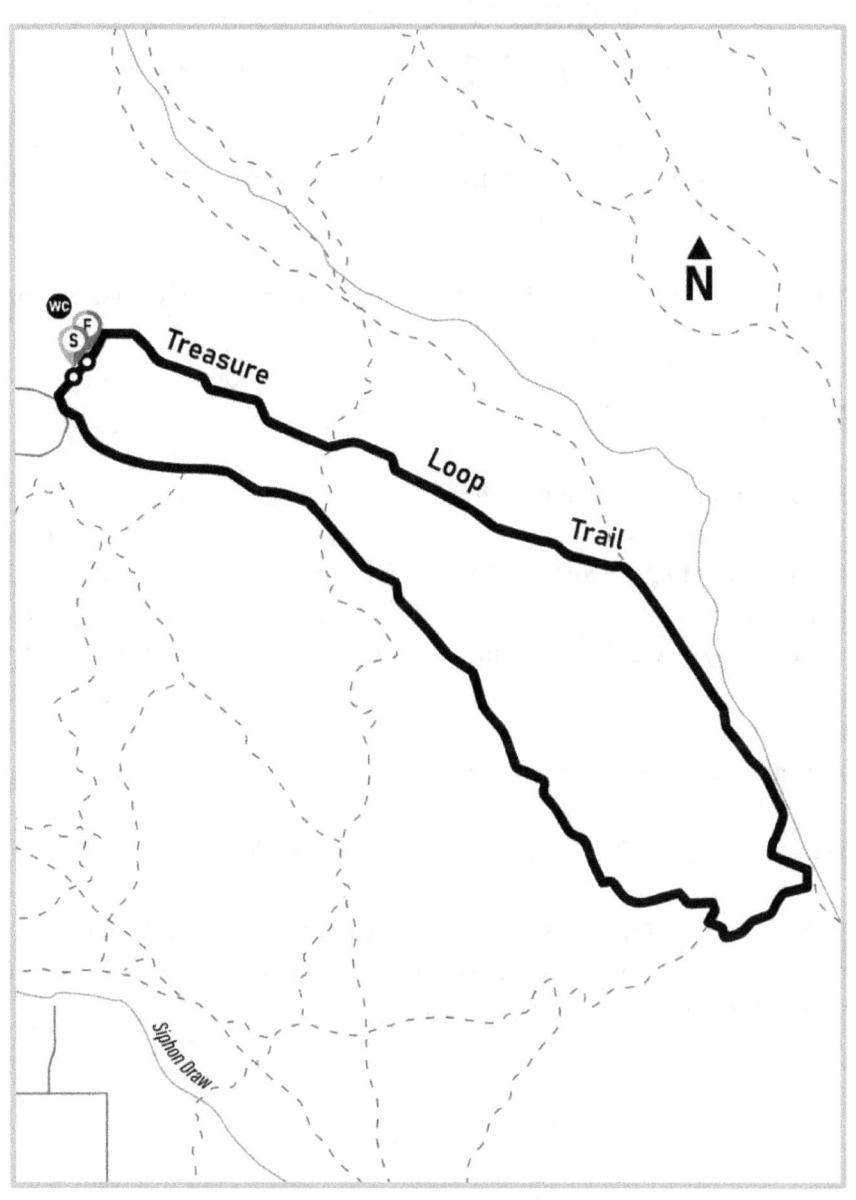

CAPE ROYAL TRAIL AT GRAND CANYON NATIONAL PARK

Cape Royal is a peninsula that extends into the Grand Canyon and is a great viewpoint of the Grand Canyon's North Rim. It is the widest panorama of any overlook.

The trail is easy (1) and short, at 0.3 miles. The path is paved and at least 5 feet wide, so it is very stroller accessible.

Best time to visit: Anytime

Pass/permit/fees: $35 per vehicle

How to get there: From Fredonia, AZ, head south on US-89A toward Lukus Ln. until AZ-67 S. Turn right onto AZ-67 S and go about 40 miles to Cape Royal Rd. Turn left and continue for 20 miles to the parking area.

Amenities: Restrooms and picnic tables near the parking lot

What to pack: Picnic lunch, camera, sun protection, water

Can you find? Angels Window and Desert View Watchtower are a natural arch and a stone tower that can be seen from Cape Royal. Read the trail marker signs for fun info along the way.

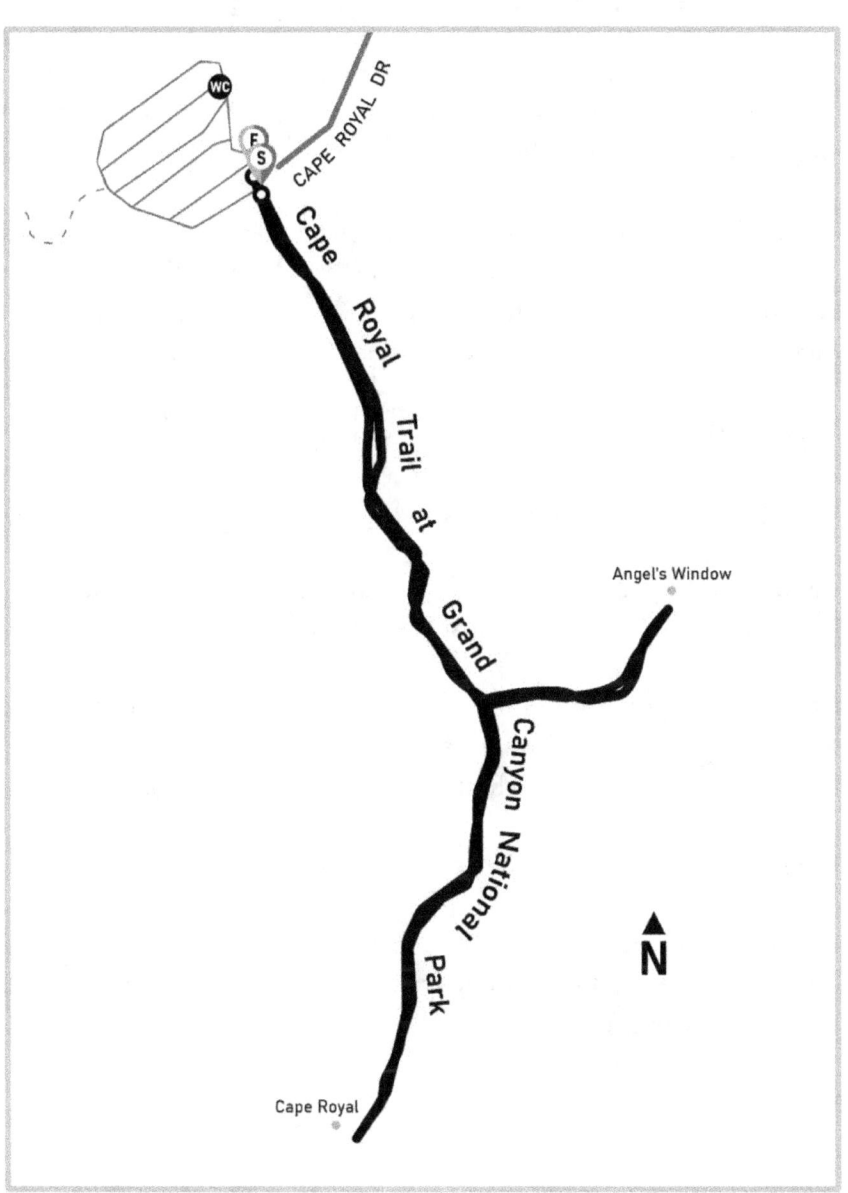

CRYSTAL FOREST TRAIL AT PETRIFIED FOREST NATIONAL PARK

The Petrified Forest has a lot of interesting things to see, such as the moon-like landscapes, the eroding badlands of the Painted Desert, and large petrified trees in rainbow hues.

Named for the lovely crystals found in petrified logs, Crystal Forest is a unique place to visit at the park. Quartz and amethyst crystals can be found within the fossilized woods. The trail is a 0.75-mile loop rated easy (1). It is also all paved, so it is stroller friendly.

Best time to visit: March-October

Pass/permit/fees: $25 per vehicle

Amenities: Restrooms and dining are available but limited. Rainbow Forest Museum is on the south side of the park.

How to get there: From Holbrook, AZ, head east on US-180 for about 17.5 miles, then turn left onto Petrified Forest Rd. The Crystal Forest trailhead will be on your right in approximately 8.1 miles.

What to pack: Sun protection, extra water, camera, snacks

Can you find? Placards about the forest are located throughout the trail. There are crystals of many colors found in the petrified wood. What colors can you spot?

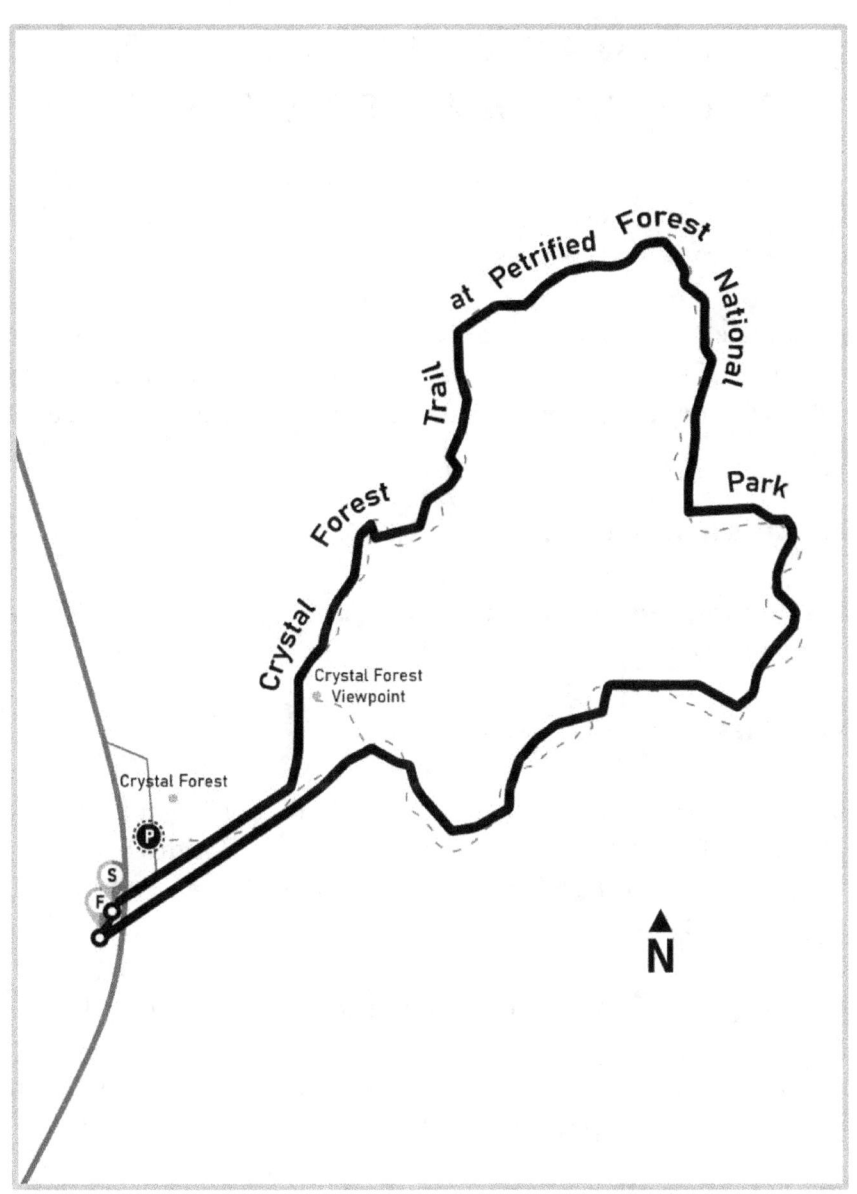

HANGING GARDEN TRAIL AT GLEN CANYON NATIONAL RECREATION AREA

This dusty red trail feels like a Martian landscape, as it's surrounded by red rock with colorful bands and mounds of sandstone. The path is lined with rocks and features glimpses of Lake Powell.

It ultimately leads to an unexpected sight of greenery within the desert, where a fern garden grows from the side of a sandstone butte from a natural spring. The trail is a 1-mile round trip and is rated easy (1).

Best time to visit: Winter, spring, fall

Pass/permit/fees: Glen Canyon National Park charges a $30 per vehicle entry fee.

Amenities: No restrooms at the trailhead

How to get there: From Page, AZ, take US-89 North and turn right before the Glen Canyon Dam. The turn-off is marked with a hiker sign. The parking lot for the trailhead will be in about 0.2 miles and on the right.

What to pack: Sun protection, water, snacks

Can you find? This green oasis is an unexpected sight in the desert, with ferns, lilies, sedges, and orchids.

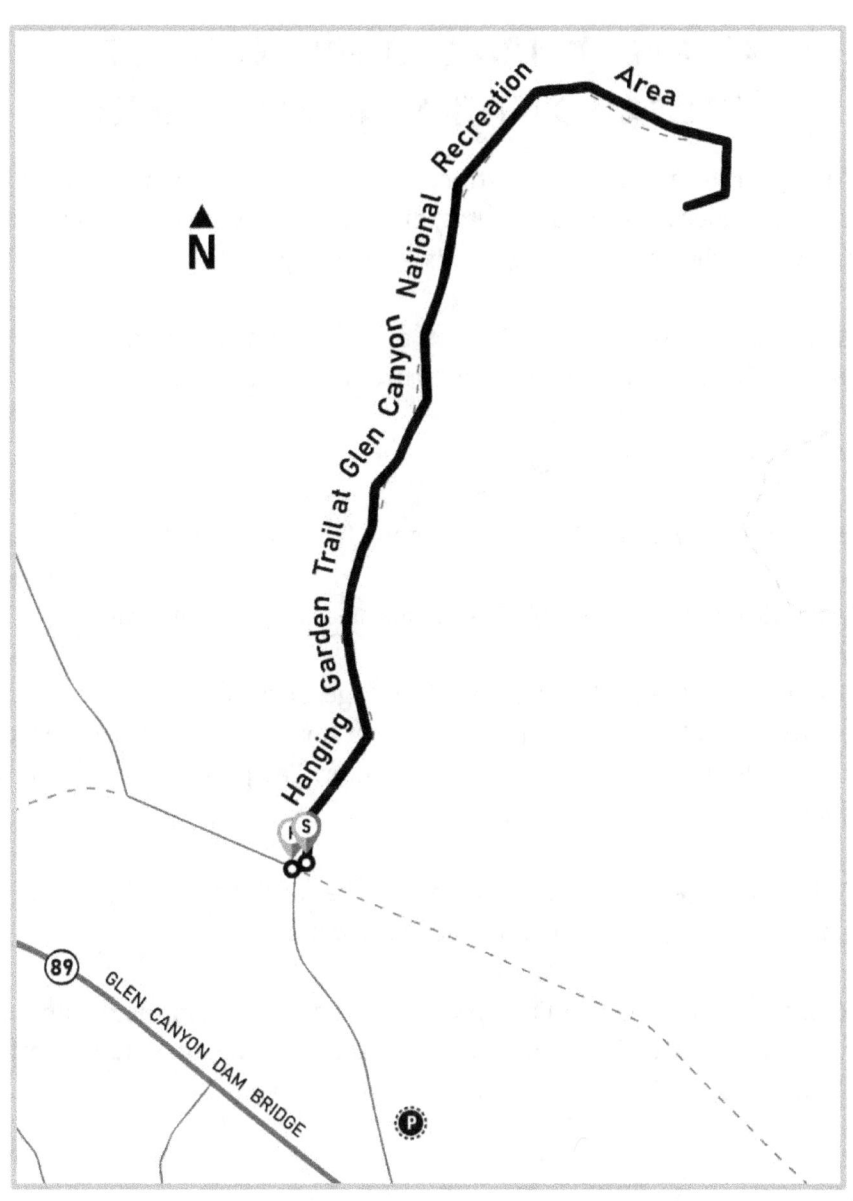

LAVA FLOW TRAIL AT SUNSET CRATER VOLCANO NATIONAL MONUMENT

Sunset Crater Volcano is an extinct cinder volcano surrounded by lava fields, pumice rocks, and hornitos, displaying evidence of the volcanic activity of the area from thousands of years ago.

The trail goes through the Bonito Lava Flow and around the base of Sunset Crater. It is a 1-mile round trip and rated easy (2).

Best time to visit: Spring, winter, fall

Pass/permit/fees: $5 per person, good for 7 days

Amenities: Restrooms are located on the east side of the trail.

How to get there: From Flagstaff, AZ, go north on US-89 for 11.9 miles, pass US-66, and continue on Loop Road for 3.5 miles. Go past the Bonito Campground and Visitor Center. The parking area will be on the south side of the road.

What to pack: Wear sturdy shoes for the loose gravel. There is no shade, so bring sun protection and extra water.

Can you find? The San Francisco Peaks can be seen in the distance. Read the signs with information about the area and enjoy the desert wildflowers and shade from the ponderosa pines.

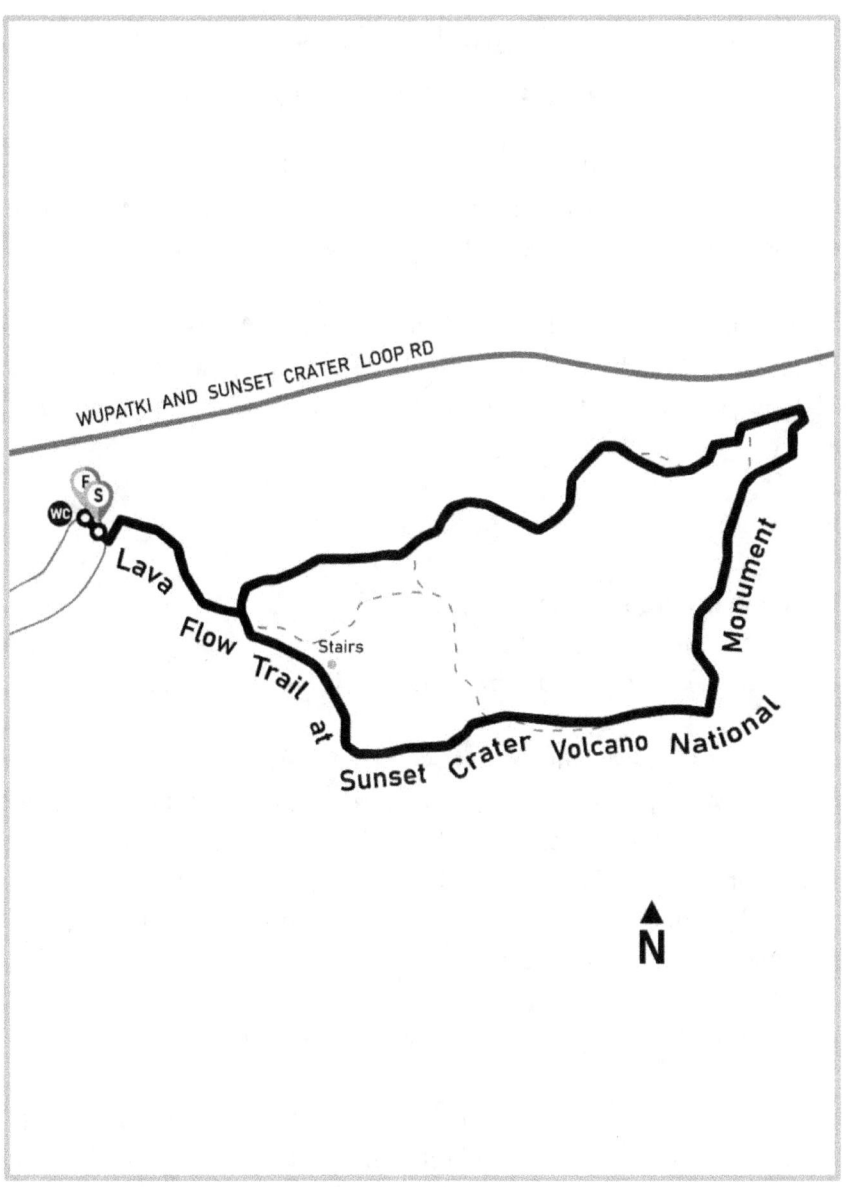

SIGNAL HILL - SAGUARO NATIONAL PARK

Rising at just over 50 feet is a minor summit in the Tucson Mountain district in Saguaro National Park. From the top are excellent views extending for over 20 miles of sloping plains.

A point of interest is also the dozens of petroglyphs carved on the rocks around the hill that were likely left during hunting expeditions. The Signal Hill Trail to the summit is 0.4 miles round trip and rated easy (1).

Best time to visit: October-April

Pass/permit/fees: $25 per vehicle

Amenities: Picnic ramadas, restroom facilities, no potable water

How to get there: From Tucson, AZ, take Speedway Blvd. west, which becomes West Gates Pass Rd., and continue to Kinney Rd. Turn right onto Kinney Rd. and pass the Red Hills Visitor Center to Hohokam Rd. Turn right onto Hohokam Rd./Bajada Loop and continue to Golden Gate Rd., looping left onto Golden Gate Rd. The picnic area and trailhead are off Golden Gate Rd.

What to pack: Extra water, sun protection, snacks

Can you find? From the summit, you can view various cacti varieties, such as the saguaro, opuntia, cholla, and ocotillo. There are also palo verde trees and petroglyphs are found in the rock around the hill.

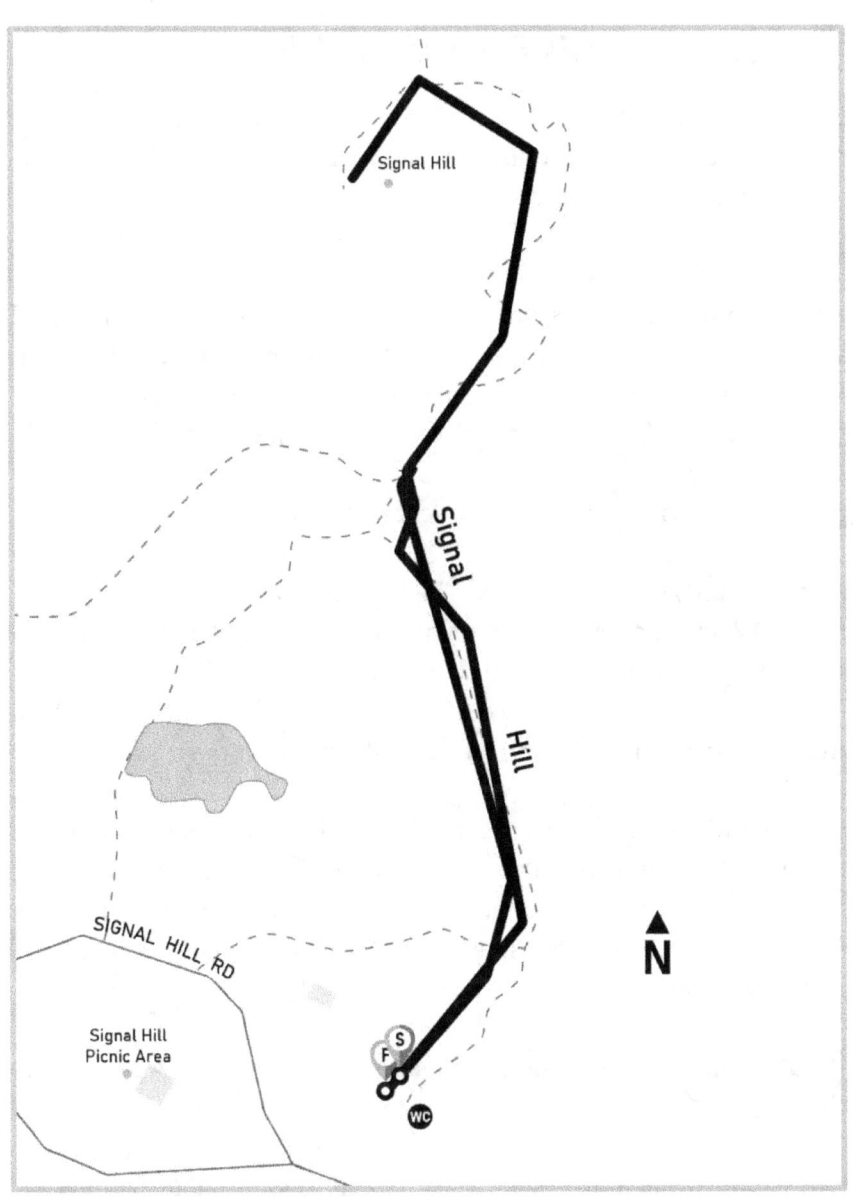

SEVEN FALLS TRAIL

One of the most popular hikes in Tucson, Seven Falls Trail boasts seven waterfalls in the middle of the Sonoran Desert. The falls are within Bear Canyon, and you get to traverse along Bear Creek and across it on your way.

It is recommended to take the tram that will take you to the trailhead, which cuts the hike in half and makes it a 4.6-mile round trip. At the falls, water cascades down the surrounding cliffs into clear pools for wading and relaxing. This trail is rated moderately easy (2.5).

Best time to visit: Late winter or early spring

Pass/permit/fees: $5 per day. The tram is $4/adult and $2/children ages 2-12 and runs every hour on the hour starting at 9 am and ending around 4 p.m. depending on the season.

Amenities: Flush toilets and water refill station at the trailhead

How to get there: From Tucson, AZ, take I-10 W to exit 256 toward Grant Rd. Continue onto Grant Rd. for about 5 miles and turn left onto N Swan Rd. Go 4 miles and turn right onto E Sunrise Dr. and go another 4 miles. Turn left onto N Sabino Canyon Rd. and the destination will be on your right.

What to pack: Water shoes, swimsuits, towels, sun protection, extra clothes/socks

Can you find? Mammals such as the javelina, whitetail deer, and road runners frequent the area.

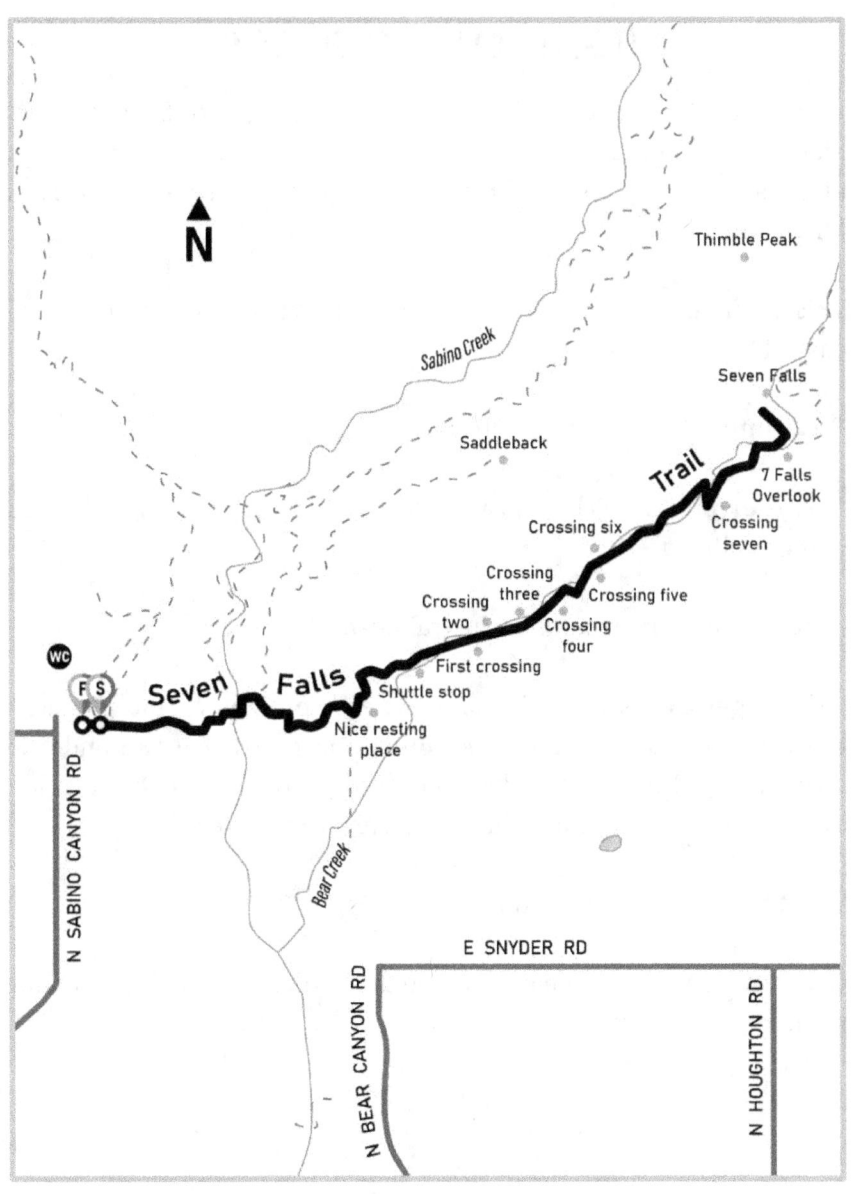

SUGARLOAF LOOP TRAIL

Located in the Coconino National Forest, this area of Sedona offers magnificent panoramas with a bird's eye view of the area from the top of Sugarloaf Mountain. Sedona is known for its beautiful red rock formations.

This 1.9-mile loop, the well-marked trail is stroller-friendly and rated easy (1).

Best time to visit: Spring, fall, winter

Pass/permit/fees: There is a $6 entry fee, though parking is limited at the trailhead.

Amenities: No restrooms at the trailhead

How to get there: From Sedona AZ, head south on N State Rte. 89A toward Forest Rd. Continue on AZ-89A until Soldiers Pass Rd. and take a right. Go 1.3 miles and take a left onto Shadow Rock Dr. Turn left onto Vista Grande Ct. and follow it to the parking area.

What to pack: Sun protection, water, snacks

Can you find? Prickly pear cacti line the hiking trail. Look around for the juniper trees, too.

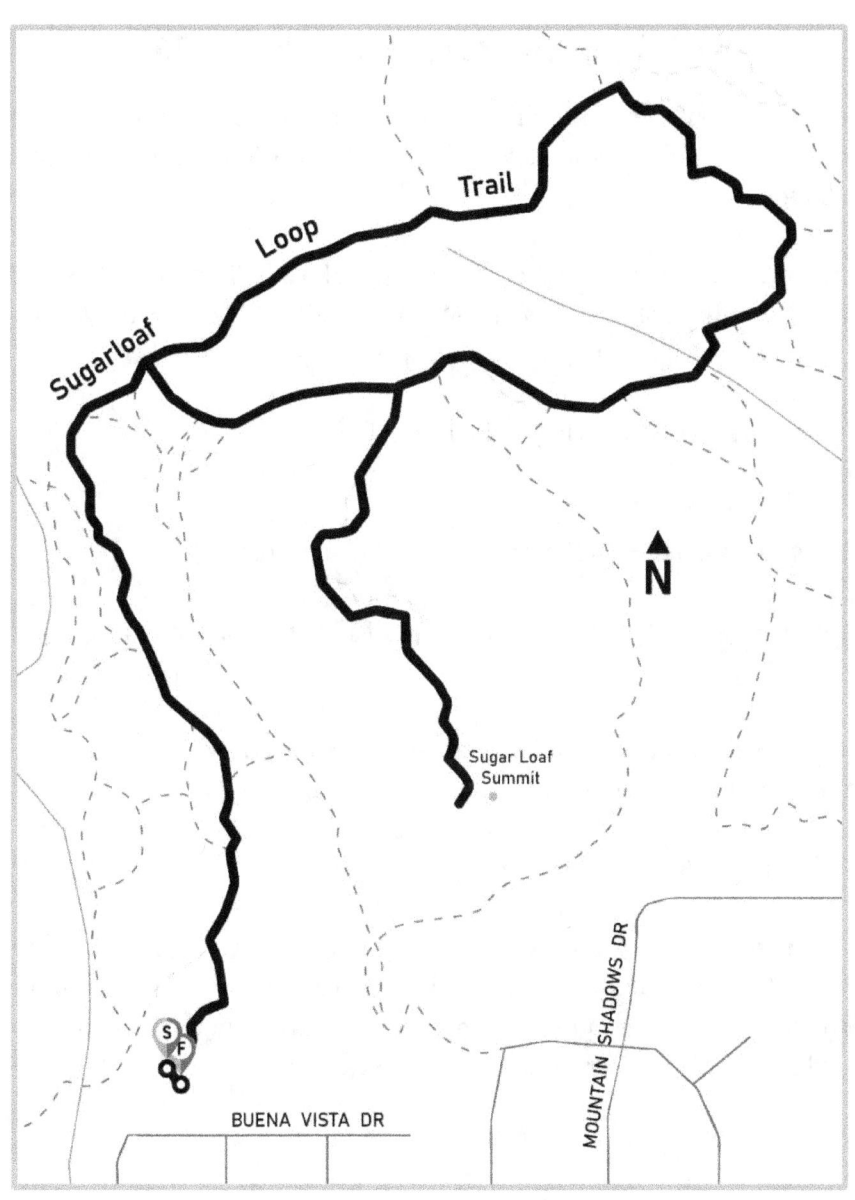

GRAND CANYON SOUTH RIM TRAIL

Generally flat, the South Rim Trail is one of the most popular hikes in the park with fantastic views of the Colorado River and the Grand Canyon.

If someone in your party gets tired, the Hermit Rest Bus stops and picks up hikers along the trail. Much of the trail is covered by trees. The entire trail is 8 miles and rated as moderately easy (2).

Best time to visit: Spring and fall

Pass/permit/fees: $35 per vehicle, good for 7 days

Amenities: Restrooms at both ends of the trail, snack bar, and gift shop

How to get there: From Flagstaff, AZ, take US-180 W to AZ-64 N. Go about 28 miles to the S Entrance Rd.

What to pack: Sun protection, water, snacks

Can you find? With the river in the canyon, there's lots of greenery to view. Can you identify coyote willow, arrow weed, seep willow, or western honey mesquite? Mammals you might spot in the canyon include bighorn sheep, mule deer, and gray foxes.

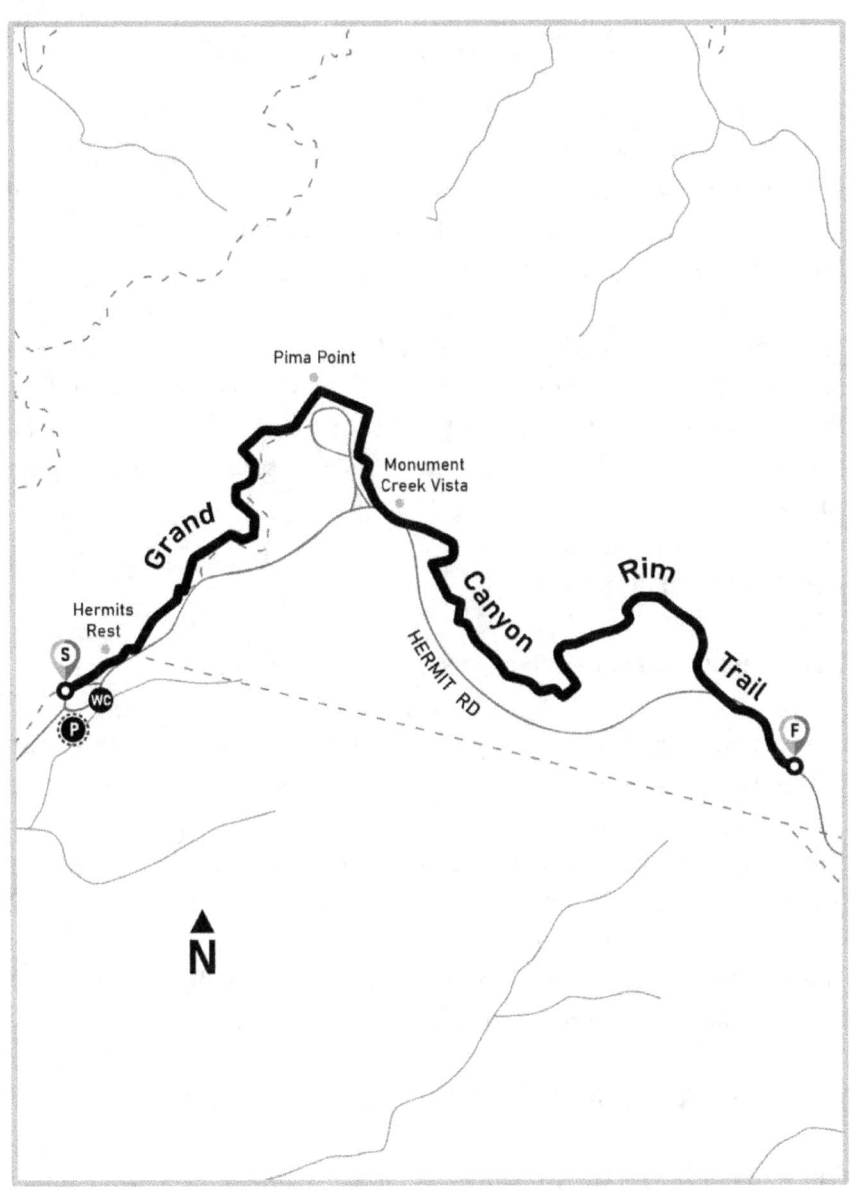

FAY CANYON TRAIL

A hike through a small, hidden canyon, this trail offers intriguing rock formations, box canyons, and gorgeous red rock scenery. There are also seasonal waterfalls throughout the canyon. The canyon is located in the scenic Sedona area full of hiking opportunities, and the trailhead is easily accessed via a paved road.

The main attraction is the natural arch, which is found within a mile into the hike on a short detour that requires some rock scrambling. Fay Canyon Trail is 2.6 miles out and back and is rated easy (1). The path is partly shaded, straightforward, and pretty level with a few mild rocky areas.

Best time to visit: Spring

Pass/permit/fees: Red Rock Pass required and are $5.

Amenities: Restrooms and picnic tables located at the trailhead parking lot

How to get there: From Sedona, AZ - Take AZ-89A S out of Sedona. At the traffic circle, take the 2nd exit to remain on AZ-89A for about 1.2 miles. Turn right onto Dry Creek Rd, and in 2 miles, continue onto Boynton Pass Rd. In about 3 miles, the parking lot will be on your left and the trailhead is across the street.

What to pack: Sturdy hiking shoes, water, camera, bear spray

Can you find? The trail includes many yucca and opuntia cacti along with wildflowers and cottonwood trees. Also look for evidence of ancient dwellings in the area.

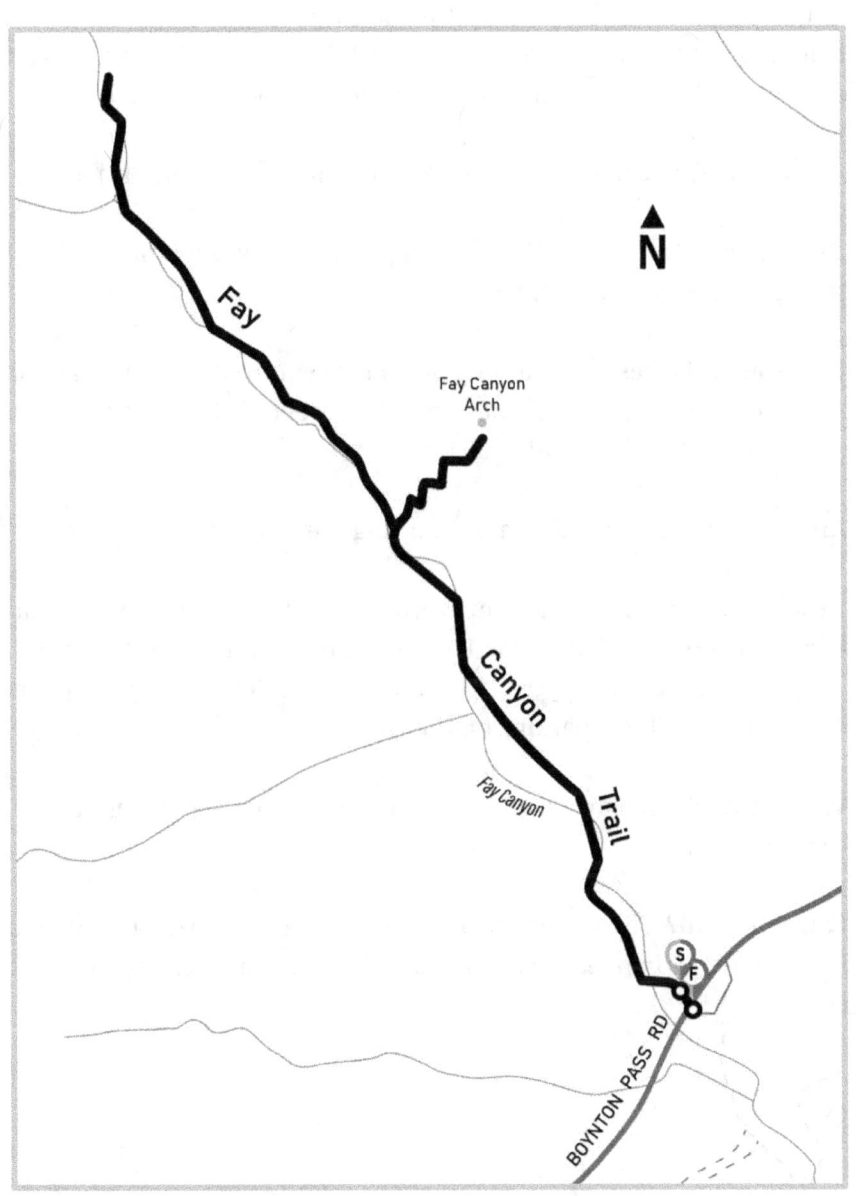

FOSSIL CREEK WATERFALL

This trail features crystal clear turquoise water set against a desert landscape in the Coconino Forest. Fossil Creek is designated a "Wild and Scenic River" and leads to a waterfall and swimming hole.

It is a little over a mile to the waterfall, making this an easy (1) journey.

Best time to visit: May or September for bearable hiking temperatures and swimming

Pass/permit/fees: $10 parking permit is required, and reservations must be made in advance from April 1-October 1. No fees or permits are required October 2-March 31.

Amenities: Port-o-potties in the parking area

How to get there: From Camp Verde, AZ, take I-17 to exit 287 and turn east on AZ-260 towards Payson. Travel 10 miles to Forest Rd. 708/Fossil Creek Rd. on the right. Go 14 miles down this bumpy dirt road to the trailhead parking on the left.

What to pack: Sun protection, water shoes, swimwear, water, towels, snacks, lunch

Can you find? The water attracts otters, beaver, Arizona toad, and leopard frogs. Unique trees to find are the Arizona alder and Fremont cottonwood.

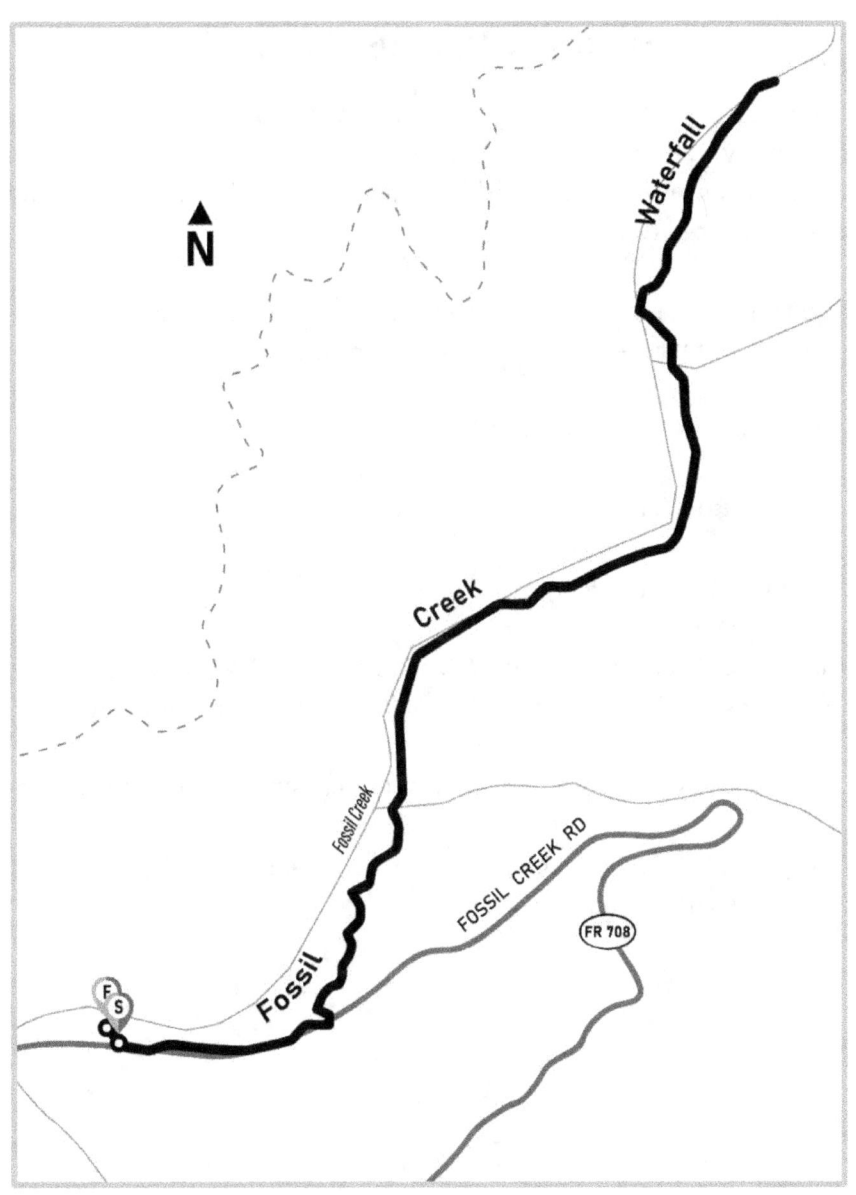

HORSESHOE BEND TRAIL

Featuring a great view of the Colorado River, the horseshoe bend is a frequently photographed feature of the river. It is a 1,000-foot drop and 270-degree bend, and the bluish-green of the river sits beautifully against the red rock.

The trail to the bend features two shade structures and is stroller-accessible. It is rated easy (1) and is 1.4 miles total round trip.

Best time to visit: Spring and fall

Pass/permit/fees: $10 per vehicle or vessel

Amenities: Vault toilet

How to get there: From Page, AZ, head south on US-89 S. The turnout for Horseshoe Bend will be on the right, between mile 544 and 545.

What to pack: Extra water, sun protection, camera, sturdy footwear

Can you find? The high cliffs surrounding the river bring eagles and falcons soaring around the area.

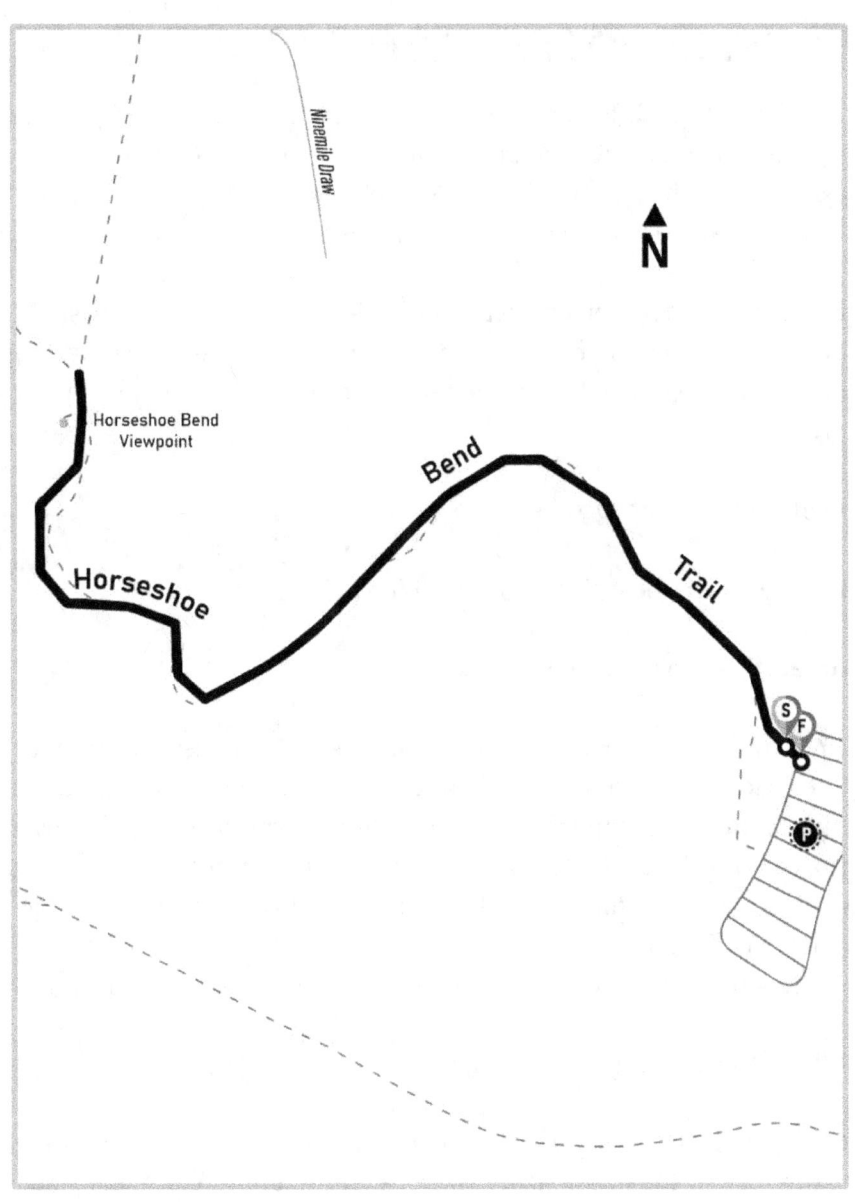

WHITE POCKET - VERMILLION CLIFFS

The Vermillion Cliffs National Monument is full of scenic, unique rock formations in amazing colors. White Pocket is a remote location to explore the amazing landscape. There's not a defined path or trail around the area, so you really can't explore.

Because access is pretty difficult, this trail is rated as medium-easy (2). Be sure to check the road conditions before departing by contacting or visiting the Kanab Visitor Center. You can also hire a guide if you'd prefer.

Best time to visit: October-June

Pass/permit/fees: No pass/permit/fees

Amenities: No restrooms or portable water

How to get there: From Kanab, Utah, take US-89 east for 39 miles. The road will curve to the right and then again to the left, but rather than taking the second curve, go straight onto the gravel road. This is House Rock Valley Rd., and there is a sign at the turnoff. Go 20.2 miles on this road until Pine Tree Rd./Road 1017. Turn left and go 6.2 miles and turn left in front of the farmhouse on Road 1087. In 3.9 miles, take the fork to the left and you will arrive at the parking area in 5.6 miles.

What to pack: Extra water, sun protection, camera, picnic lunch

Can you find? Petroglyphs are featured here, and in one area is a cattle trail of indentations in the rock. The Monolith is a giant rock formation in the distance, and the Swirl has stripes of colorful rock rising toward the sky.

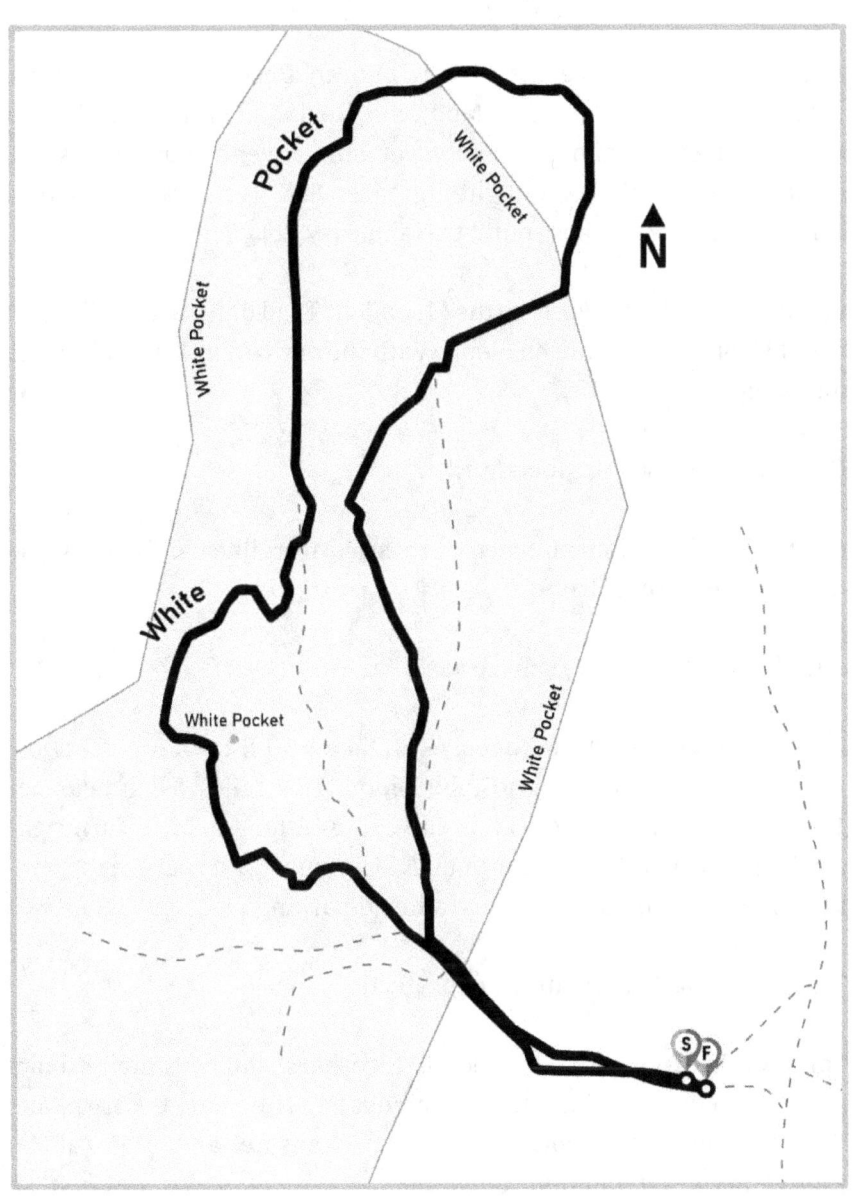

MOONLIGHT-STARGAZER-SAN TAN TRAIL

Hikers will experience the lower Sonoran Desert on this popular desert trail in the San Tan Mountain Regional Park. There are a handful of trails, and a friendly yet still adventurous one is the combination of the Moonlight-Stargazer-San Tan Trail. This trail combination is 2.3 miles round trip and easy (2).

For an even milder hike, take the Moonlight Trail only, at 1.3 miles and easy (1), or opt for more challenge with the entire San Tan Trail, at 5.1 miles and moderate (3).

Best time to visit: October-April

Amenities: Restroom and picnic areas are at trailheads. There is also the San Tan Nature Center.

Pass/permit/fees: $7/vehicle entry fee

How to get there: From Phoenix, AZ, take I-10 E to US-60 E. Follow signs for Mesa/Globe/Mesa-Globe and go 18.7 miles. Then take exit 190B for AZ-202 S and go 3 miles to exit 34A for AZ-24 E. Turn right onto S Ellsworth Rd. and continue N. Thompson Rd. Turn right onto W. Phillips Rd. and drive to the trailhead parking.

What to pack: Extra water, sun protection, snacks

Can you find? Javelinas, curved bill thrashers, and cottontail rabbits might be seen traveling through the desert. The usual desert plants such as saguaros, choola, barrel cacti, creosote, and sage can be spotted in the surrounding landscape.

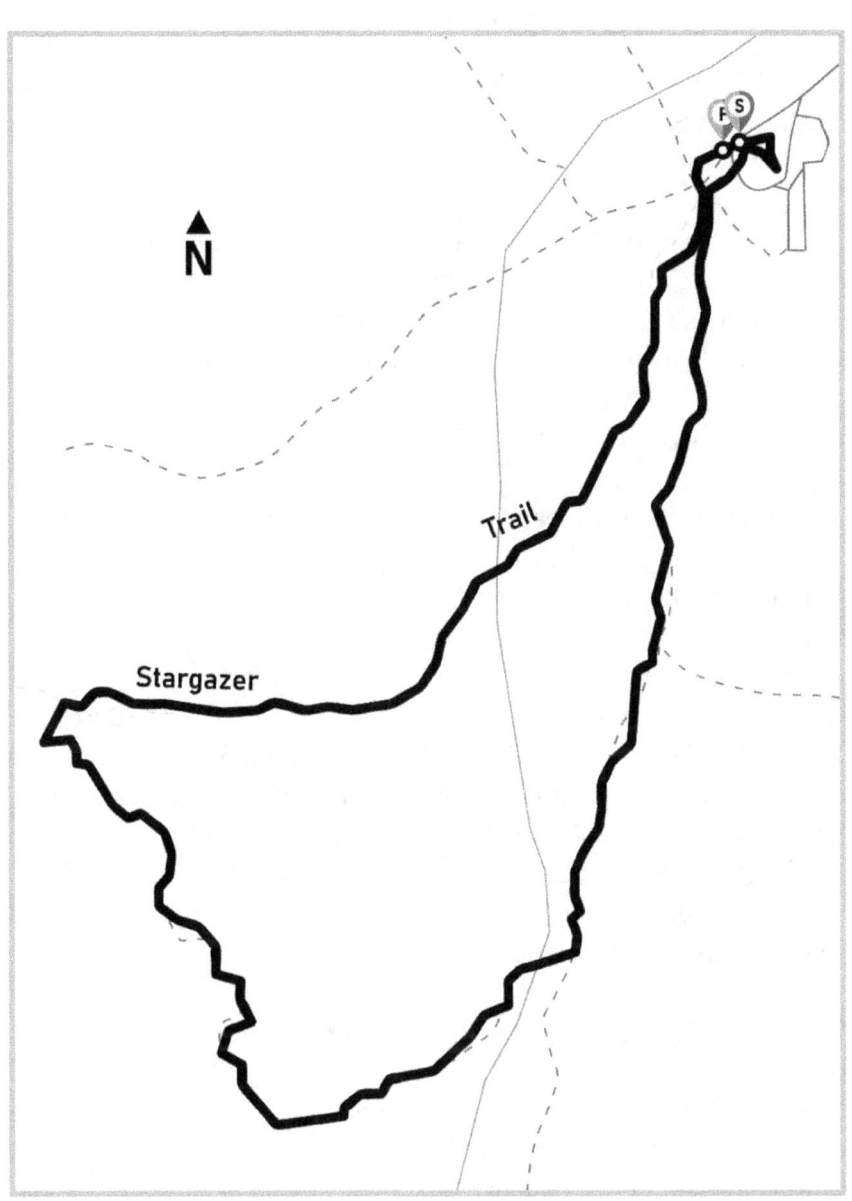

PINNACLE PEAK

Pinnacle Peak Trail is 3.5 miles round trip. This out-and-back trail has an elevation gain of about 1,300 feet, with rock climbing available for those with the ability.

This trail can be quite busy at times, so give those climbing the right of way. There are a couple of good spots to appreciate the beautiful view from the trail, despite the trail not leading all the way to the summit of the mountain. This trail is easy-moderate (2).

Best time to visit: Spring or fall

Pass/permit/fees: No pass, permit, or fee required

Amenities: Drinking fountains and restrooms are located at the trailhead.

How to get there: From Phoenix, AZ, get on I-10 E toward Tucson. Take Exit 147A-147B for AZ-51 N. Continue on AZ-51 N for 14.9 miles and take Exit 15A to merge onto AZ-101 Loop E. Go 4.3 miles and take Exit 34 for Scottsdale Rd. and turn left. Go 4.8 miles and turn right onto E Jomax Rd. Continue 2 miles and turn left onto N Pima Rd. After 1 mile, turn right at the first cross street onto E Dynamite Rd. and continue 3 miles. Then turn left onto N Alma School Pkwy.

What to pack: Water, snacks, sun protection

Can you find? Many critters can be seen here, such as quail, jackrabbits, cactus wren, antelope ground squirrels, scampering lizards, roadrunner, and mule deer.

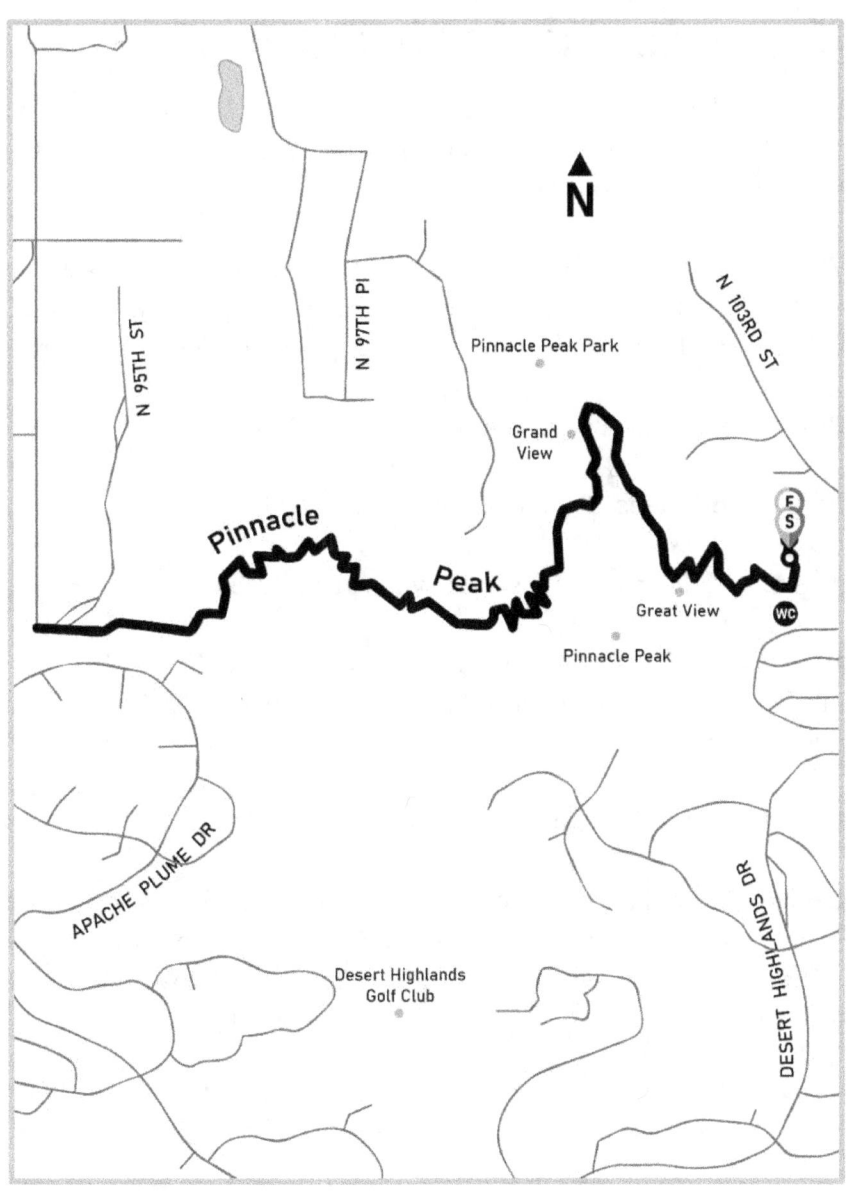

THE WIND CAVE TRAIL IN EAST MESA

Enjoy the beautiful view of the valley from the top of this trail. The Wind Cave trail is shorter — only 3 miles. With an elevation of 810 feet, the trail is considered easy (2).

The only stop on the trail is at the top, in the small "cave" for which the trail is named. The cave, despite being small, offers hikers a place to rest and recover before the trip back down the trail.

Best time to visit: Between April and November

Pass/permit/fees: $7/day-use entry pass

Amenities: The trailhead is equipped with restrooms.

How to get there: From Phoenix, AZ, take I-10 E to US 60 E. Take the Ellsworth Rd. exit, then follow Ellsworth Rd./Usery Pass Rd. north to the User Mountain Regional Park entrance.

What to pack: Water, snacks, possibly a headlamp

Can you find? Many desert cacti like the saguaro and prickly pear are found here, along with palo verde trees. There are also various types of lizards and sometimes the odd snake, horned toad, or desert tortoise.

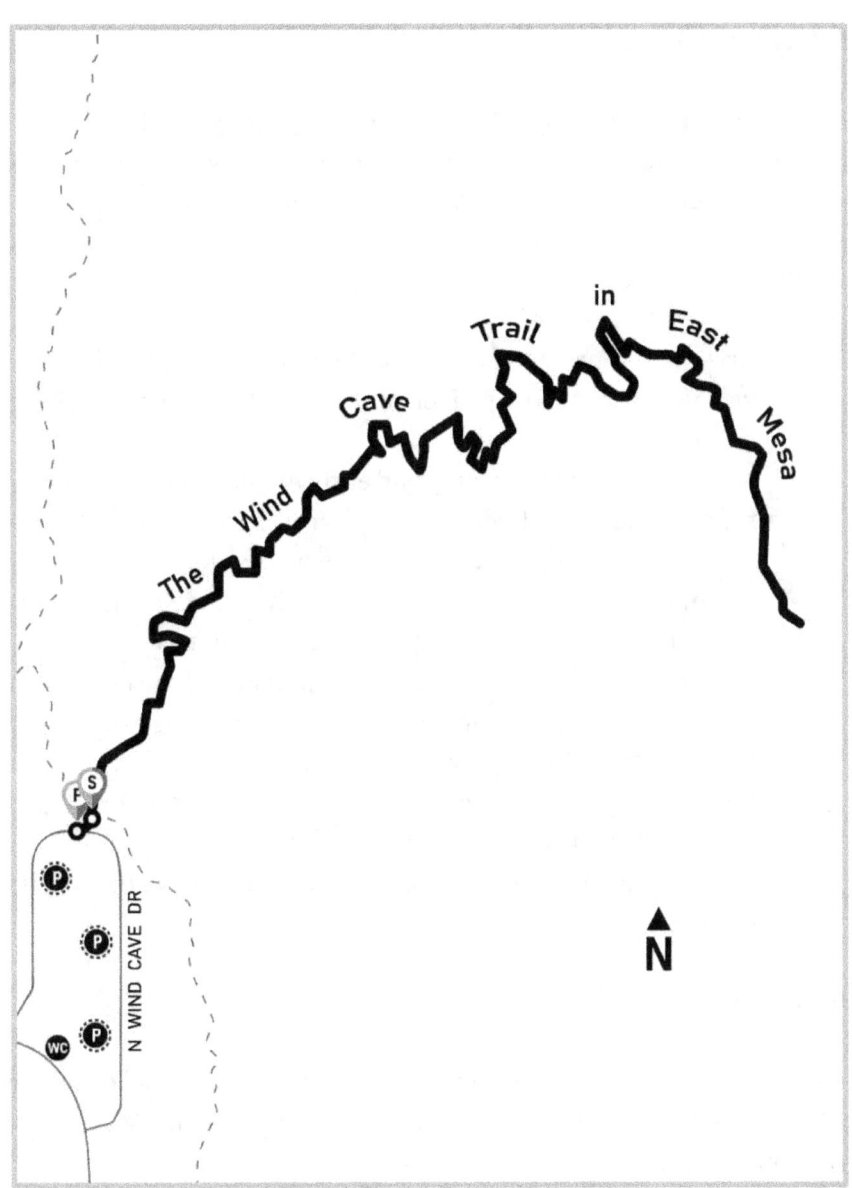

Safety Guidelines

Before embarking on any family adventures, safety first! To ensure you and your family create amazing memories, review these safety warnings regularly to prepare for Arizona's weather and wildlife.

Weather Conditions

- Arizona is prone to wildfires, so always check for any warnings and follow proper procedures to prevent causing a wildfire.
- Monsoon season is late July and early August and brings heavy rainfall and flash flooding. Be aware of the forecast before departing on a hike and keep an eye on the skies.
- Arizona experiences extreme weather, so prepare for extremely hot and extremely cold temperatures.
- The hot temperatures of Arizona summers and the desert can cause serious, heat-related illnesses. Always bring extra water for everyone and keep hydrated.
- Keep your bodies fueled with good meals before your hike, salty snacks during your hike, and an ample meal post-hike.
- Dust storms might occur. Keep masks/bandanas around just in case.

Dangerous Wildlife

There are several dangerous animals and insects you may encounter while hiking in Arizona. With a good dose of caution and awareness, you can explore safely.

Venomous animals and insects such as rattlesnakes, Sonoran Desert toad scorpions, tarantula hawks, kissing bugs, Arizona Giant Centipedes, Gila monsters, spiders, and tarantulas are found in Arizona. Luckily, only a few are truly life-threatening and bites are rare occurrences.

There are also predatory animals such as coyotes, cougars, mountain lions, and black bears found in the Grand Canyon State. These animals tend to avoid areas with humans and can often be enjoyed from afar with a pair of binoculars.

There are also various species of flora that are poisonous or harmful. The jumping cholla cactus is the most likely issue and is easily avoidable by maintaining a safe distance. If any cactus stems get stuck to your body, a comb or tweezers are effective for removal.

Here is what you can do to keep yourself and your loved ones safe from dangerous flora and fauna while exploring Arizona:
- Keep to the established trails.
- Do not look under rocks, leaves, or sticks.
- Keep hands and feet out of small crawl spaces, bushes, covered areas, or crevices.
- Wear long sleeves and pants to keep arms and legs protected.
- Keep your distance should you encounter any dangerous wildlife or plants.

Limited Cell Service

Do not rely on cell service for navigation or emergencies. Always have a map with you and let someone know where you are and for how long you intend to be gone, just in case.

First Aid Information

Always travel with a first aid kit with you in case of emergencies. Here are items to be certain to include in your primary first aid kit:
- Nitrile gloves
- Blister care products
- Band-aids - multiple sizes and waterproof type
- Ace wrap and athletic tape

- Alcohol wipes and antibiotic ointment
- Irrigation syringe
- Tweezers, nail clippers, trauma shears, safety pins
- Small Ziplock bags for containing contaminated trash

It is recommended to also keep a secondary first aid kit for more serious injuries or medical emergencies. Items in this should include:
- Blood clotting sponges
- Sterile gauze pads
- Trauma pads
- Second-skin/burn treatment
- Triangular bandages/sling
- Butterfly strips
- Tincture of benzoin
- Medications (ibuprofen, acetaminophen, antihistamine, aspirin, etc.)
- Thermometer
- CPR mask
- Wilderness medicine handbook
- Antivenin

Annual Pass Information

If you live in or plan to visit Arizona frequently within a year, it might be worth your money to invest in an annual pass. The Arizona State Parks have two annual pass options to consider.

Arizona State Parks - Standard Annual Pass

The Standard Annual Pass allows non-commercial day-use access at Arizona State Parks for pass holders and up to three additional adults in the same vehicle, except for daily entry to Boyce Thompson Arboretum and Lake Havasu, Cattail Cove, Buckskin Mountain, and River Island State Parks on weekends (Fridays, Saturdays, and Sundays) and state holidays from April 1 to October 31.

$75 plus a $7 handling fee

Arizona State Parks - Premium Annual Pass

An Arizona State Parks Premium Annual Pass provides non-commercial day-use access at all Arizona State Parks for the pass holder and up to three additional adults in the same vehicle, with the exception of the Boyce Thompson Arboretum.

Choose this pass if you want to include access to Lake Havasu, Cattail Cove, Buckskin Mountain, and River Island State Parks on weekends and state holidays from April 1 to October 31.

$200 plus a $7 handling fee

America the Beautiful
The National Parks and Federal Recreational Lands Pass Series

The "America the Beautiful Pass" is accepted at many of the locations listed in this book. Entrance fees at national parks and national wildlife refuges as well as standard amenity fees (day use fees) at national forests and grasslands are covered under the pass. Also, lands managed by the Bureau of Land Management, Bureau of Reclamation, and the U.S. Army Corps of Engineers are included in the pass. A pass covers fees for a driver and all passengers in a personal vehicle or up to four adults at sites that charge per person. Children aged 15 or under are admitted for free.

- $80 General Annual Pass
- $80 Lifetime Senior Pass (ages 62 or over)
- $20 Annual Senior Pass (ages 62 or over)
- Free Access Pass for U.S. citizens or permanent residents with permanent disabilities

- Free Military Pass for current U.S. military members, U.S. military veterans, and Gold Star Family Members
- Free Fourth Grade Pass for U.S. fourth-graders for the duration of the school year through the following summer
- Free Volunteer Pass for volunteers with over 250 service hours with federal agencies that participate in the Interagency Pass Program (National Park Service, U.S. Forest Service, U.S. Fish, and Wildlife Service, Bureau of Land Management, Bureau of Reclamation, U.S. Army Corps of Engineers)

www.ingramcontent.com/pod-product-compliance
Lightning Source LLC
Chambersburg PA
CBHW071458070526
44578CB00001B/384